D1166753

The WonderWeeks

Milestone Guide

Your Baby's Development, Sleep, and Crying Explained

This book is dedicated to our sweethearts:
Thomas, Victoria, Sarah and Seth.
May you have roots to grow and wings to fly.

Copyright © Kiddy World Publishing
10 9 8 7 6 5 4 3 2
Written by Xaviera Plas and Frans Plooij
Internal Design by Andrei Andras
Cover Design by Sumedia
Illustrations by Hetty van de Rijt, Vladimir Schmeisser

ISBN/EAN: 978-94-9188217-3

This book is intended as a reference volume only, not as a medical manual. The information given here is designed to help you make informed decisions about your baby's health. It is not intended as a substitute for any treatment that may have been prescribed by your doctor. If you suspect a medical problem, we urge you to seek competent medical help. Mention of specific companies, organizations, or authorities in this book does not imply endorsement by the publisher, nor does mention of specific companies, organizations, or authorities imply that they endorse this book.

All rights reserved. No part of this publication may be reproduced or transmitted in any form or by any means, electronic or mechanical, including photocopying, recording or any other information storage and retrieval system, without written permission of the publisher.

Kiddy World Publishing
Van Pallandtstraat 63
6814 GN Arnhem
The Netherlands

WWW.THEWONDERWEEKS.COM

Worldwide
best-selling
baby app

Contents

CHAPTER 2 Physical Development   33

CHAPTER 7 Stress   **119**

This Book is Gender-Neutral

We are very proud that this book has been written in gender-neutral language. There are no references to 'him' or 'her' but we use 'they' to refer to both boys and girls. You may need to get used to this when reading the book, but this enables us to emphasize what we stand for, and that applies to girls and boys: *a smart start for a happy beginning.*

Congratulations!

You've become a proud mother or father (again) of a cute baby. For months, you've been longing for the moment when you would finally hold your baby in your arms, cuddle and talk to your child, and admire their tiny feet.

There's nothing better than becoming parents. From now on, you are a team, a great unity. You want to do everything right, which brings, no doubt, a whole bunch of worries and questions with it. The questions and doubts are perfectly normal. They are even good to have. They bring out the best in you, and this is to your baby's advantage. Over the years, parents have asked me lots of questions on all kinds of subjects. They are questions that are not only on these parents' minds but that are interesting to every father and mother. I hope to answer all of your questions with this book.

Happy reading!

Definitions

Growth Spurt

- ✓ You talk about a growth spurt when the body, or a part of the body, suddenly becomes bigger or changes. Sometimes, children grow several millimeters a night and then, for a while, not at all.

- ✓ "Children grow like weeds" goes the saying, and they really do.

- ✓ The head circumference grows in spurts as well.

- ✓ The head circumference's first three growth spurts after birth coincide with the first three leaps in the baby's mental development.

- ✓ Other growth spurts rarely concur with leaps because they occur much more frequently. The baby also doesn'tstart teething during a leap.

Leap

A leap is a sudden change in the baby's mental development. Usually, it comes with the same symptoms every time; your baby is especially clingy, whiny, and moody. Leaps announce progress. In healthy children, they occur 10 times within the first 20 months after birth at approximately the same age. They are more intense in some

children than in others. Every leap brings a change in the brain, broadening the perceptive ability by another skill.

Skills

When a child's cognitive ability increases with a leap, he or she is able to learn a whole bunch of new skills and new behavior that the child didn't know before since the brain wasn't ready for it then. The new behavior is the result of tireless work. It doesn't just fall into the child's lap, but the baby has to work hard for it. Every skill requires practicing, and practicing requires time. Your baby starts the process of acquiring a new skill when it suits him or her. The child makes the call and can't acquire all skills at the same time. That's why the age when a new behavior appears varies from child to child.

Perceptive ability

Each leap brings your baby a new cognitive ability. It is a present to the baby, who doesn't have to do anything to receive it. Within the first 20 months, your baby acquires 10 cognitive abilities. Each extension of the cognitive ability is the result of a sudden change in the brain. It happens at around the same age for every child. Each extension of the cognitive ability provides the baby with a brand-new option to learn. This means that your baby is able to learn a whole new range of skills. These skills are all due to the new perceptive ability, and the baby couldn't have learned them before the appearance of the new perceptive ability. The new perceptive abilities that are, one by one, available to the baby during the first 20 months are "sensations," "patterns," "smooth transitions," "events," "relationships," "categories," "sequences," "programs," "principles," and "systems." These perceptive abilities are explained in detail in the book, The Wonder Weeks.

CHAPTER 1

Mental Development

Leaps, Working the Brain, Clinginess,
Fusiness, and Moodiness

As parents, you are very interested in what happens inside your baby's little head. What does a baby experience? How is the child feeling? What does or doesn't a baby understand? Why does a baby consider something to be very funny? Of course, you can't ask your child yet, so all you can do is read their behavior and body language. Knowing your baby's mental development makes it a lot easier to understand your baby.

Why is mental development so important?

We tend to mainly look at visible results. Is the baby able to walk? Are they able to talk? Of course, it's great to experience the first milestone, but the process that takes place *before* the milestone is really what's important and interesting. In order to be able to perform an action, no matter what it is, the brain has to be able to communicate with the body. The brain has to be capable of receiving signals from the outside world, translating them, and then stimulating the body to "do something." If the brain is not capable of receiving signals from the outside world, it can't translate them nor stimulate the body. Adults, for instance, know that you have to lift your foot to climb a step because you know that the step is higher up than the floor you're standing on. Little babies don't understand the consequences of height differences, yet. Babies see the step but don't understand what a step requires until the brain develops this ability during a mental leap. Once the mental leap is complete, babies are suddenly better able to handle height differences. As a mom or a dad, you see the outcome, and you're proud of it. Your baby is able to do something new. However, it is very important to realize that the true milestone happened in the brain during mental development. Everything we do and know is determined by our mental development.

What exactly is a leap, anyway?

A leap in your baby's mental development means a big, sudden change in your baby's little head. The brain is now capable of perceiving things that it couldn't perceive before. The change is so large that the baby's whole world seems different now.

How does my baby's world change when they take a leap in their mental development?

With each leap your baby takes, they acquire a new cognitive ability. This new ability enables your baby to perceive, see, hear, taste, smell, and feel new things. Everything your baby notices now is new even though it has been in their surroundings for quite a while. Your baby hasn't noticed it until now because their brain wasn't able to understand it. From the moment your baby takes the leap, this changes, and suddenly, your baby sees all the new things surrounding them. It's difficult for adults to imagine, but the baby's whole world changes because of it.

How do babies react to a leap?

During a leap, a baby's world is briefly turned upside down. The best way to describe it is to compare it to waking up on a different planet. You open your eyes, and everything has changed. What would you do? Frightened, you hang on to what you're used to and what you know. Slowly, you start exploring the new planet. That's exactly what your baby does. Your baby hangs on to you, appearing clingy. However, you don't only see the effect of a leap in your baby's exaggerated clinginess, but you'll also notice more mood swings and crying. Clinginess, whininess, and moodiness are the constant companions of every leap your child takes.

Do Remember

If all these definitions are making you dizzy, turn to page 14, chapter "Definitions."

What are the consequences for a baby of acquiring a new cognitive ability?

The new ability your baby gains during a leap gives your baby the potential to develop a whole series of skills, which can be divided into different groups according to their similarities. Compare it to a supermarket with different departments containing related products. Your baby is able to enter a certain department at a supermarket for the first time. You have to choose a product, and you can't buy everything in that department all at once. *What* your baby chooses and *how* your baby uses it is what makes your baby unique.

Is my baby going to master everything right away after taking a leap in their development?

When your baby has taken a leap in development, it means they have made room for a new cognitive ability. Your baby is not as whiny, clingy, or moody any more. Of course, this doesn't mean your baby masters every single one of the skills the new ability allows. Your baby's little brain is basically ready for a whole range of new behavior, but this requires practice. Your baby learns by experiencing, by making mistakes, and by trying tirelessly. Practice takes a lot of time. Your baby is able to master some of the skills shortly after the leap but others take longer. The skills children can master shortly after the leap are different for each baby.

What do you need to consider when your child is processing a leap?

After a leap has taken place, it has to be processed first. This is the period of time during which your baby tries to get a grip on the new possibilities. During this phase, parents learn a lot about their child's personality. Pay attention to the following:

- ✓ How does your baby handle being unsuccessful when trying something?

- ✓ Which of the new things does your baby find the most interesting and learn the quickest?

How do babies handle being unsuccessful when trying something new?

After a leap, your baby will try out all kinds of new things pertaining to the extended cognitive ability, but of course, your baby will not try all of them at once. Often, your baby will wait months between trying new things. Needless to say, not all the attempts the child makes to try and master a skill are successful. The saying "practice makes perfect" also applies to babies. One baby patiently tries over and over until they are successful. Another baby quickly gets mad and frustrated when something doesn't work out and doesn't try again. Another baby reacts with frustration if unsuccessful but eagerly keeps trying until it works. Additionally, there are many more reactions to an initially unsuccessful attempt. If you pay attention to the course of attempts, you'll see part of your baby's personality shimmer through. You'll get an idea of how your child handles failure and achieving goals. The behavior is very revealing, especially since your child hasn't learned to behave reasonably yet. Babies don't pull themselves together, don't swallow anger, and react in a very primitive manner.

When your baby processes a leap, write down how they practice their new skills. The left-hand side of the bar indicates that your baby goes about trying something new in an even-tempered frame of mind without losing their patience, while the right-hand side indicates a pretty high degree of frustration. When your baby is processing a leap, color the part of the bar that you think describes your baby. Be as unbiased as possible. Your baby's ability to handle something with patience has its advantages, but your baby is also justified in losing their patience and being frustrated. Therefore, one type of behavior is not better than the other.

Leap 1, Changing Sensations: 5 Weeks

even tempered	frustrated

Leap 2, Patterns: 8 Weeks

even tempered	frustrated

Leap 3, Smooth Transitions: 12 Weeks

even tempered	frustrated

Leap 4, Events: 19 Weeks

even tempered	frustrated

Leap 5, Relationships: 26 Weeks

even tempered	frustrated

Leap 6, Categories: 37 Weeks

even tempered	frustrated

Leap 7, Sequences: 46 Weeks

even tempered	frustrated

Leap 8, Programs: 55 Weeks

even tempered	frustrated

Leap 9, Principles: 64 Weeks

even tempered	frustrated

Leap 10, Systems: 75 Weeks

even tempered	frustrated

Which one of the new skills do babies find the most interesting?

This book tells you what your baby can learn during each individual leap. With each leap in development, a baby acquires a whole range of new possibilities. A baby is able to do and understand so many new things that only one can be selected at a time. It's simply impossible to practice and master them all at the same time. Once again, use the supermarket for comparison. Hundreds of products are being offered there. Which ones do you put in your shopping basket? You reach for the products that appeal to you. Your baby does the same thing when processing a leap. Among all the skills that are being offered, your baby picks the ones that are appealing; in other words, your baby picks the ones they have a preference for. Your baby's preferences always reveal something about their personality.

How do you discover your child's personality?

You get a pretty good picture of their personality by being responsive to everything your baby "tells" you through their body language and by carefully observing your baby. If, on top of that, you document what your baby chooses from the "supermarket" of possibilities, you get an even better picture. Some parents tend to put everything their baby is able to do on their "must-have list," which is a shame because it makes it seem like having to fill the shopping cart is the priority. It really isn't about crossing off as many skills as possible, but instead, it's about tracking your baby's preferences (also see chapter 8, "Intelligence," page 133).

What phase follows processing a leap?

The next leap comes shortly after your baby has processed the previous leap to a certain degree, and has learned a number of new skills. Your baby's life changes drastically once again. This happens 10 times during the first 20 months, mainly within the first three months as leaps are more frequent during this period. Of course, your baby is far from mastering all the potential skills of the previous leap when the next leap begins. No reason to worry, though; your baby simply continues mastering skills and doesn't pay attention to the new leap. Therefore, completely processing all the potential skills of one leap overlaps a series of other leaps.

Once my baby has mastered a skill, does it ever change again?

A new cognitive ability acquired with a new leap enables your baby to improve a previously mastered skill or to do more with it. You could compare it to building a house. First, you build the foundations and then the walls and then the roof, and finally, you divide the house into rooms and furnish it. You can't put a roof on a house that doesn't have walls. Your baby builds on the foundations of mental development. With every leap, your baby adds a level.

Your baby not only learns more skills per leap but also learns that the skills they have already acquired can be used in different ways. With every leap, a child learns to use their previous accomplishments in a more creative way. Take, for example, "grabbing." The first time your baby was able to grab hold of something it was a pretty tedious affair and with little control. Your baby's movements seemed robot-like. You were holding the toy and made sure baby's hand could get close to the toy.

A few leaps later, your baby reached for an object lying around and moved it to a different place. As you can see, grabbing has turned into a resource. Grabbing itself is not the goal any more but a means to achieve something else. The end goal has moved up a level. Baby's little hand now makes smooth movements, and your baby understands how to "navigate." The skills your baby has acquired while processing a leap have been refined (see also chapter 2, "Physical Development," page 33).

When do children take a leap in their development?

All children take their leaps at the same age. Always take the calculated date of delivery, the due date, as the starting point. It's about brain development. Whether your baby was born a few weeks earlier or later, brain development simply proceeds. The chart below shows when your child will take a leap.

How come all children take a leap at the same time? Every child is different, right?

All children take leaps at the same age because the leap's trigger comes from the inside; leaps are not influenced by children's surroundings. This doesn't mean that all children handle each leap in the same manner. Every child handles the newly acquired expansion of perceptual ability differently, which is exactly what makes each child unique.

Do I have to adjust my schedule accordingly if a new leap is about to happen?

Your child will certainly not feel well during a leap. However, the severity of bewilderment is hard to estimate. Since your child takes so many leaps during the first two years, you won't always be able to take time off during that time, of course. It's not necessary, but you should be somewhat considerate. For example, don't make an appointment for shots at the pediatrician's office during the days of a leap. If you can schedule important appointments before or after a leap, you should do so.

How come you can clearly tell when some babies are taking leaps but not others?

You can look at a leap in terms of a big change. Some adults have a stronger reaction to changes in life than others. It's the same with babies. To some children, handling changes comes naturally and is easier than it is for others. Besides temperament, these influencing factors play a role as well:

- ✓ Stressful situations

- ✓ Health

- ✓ If you are, for example, in the middle of moving your family, if your daily life is influenced by some other stressful event, or if your baby is sick, the leap is overcast by these circumstances. Your baby will be especially clingy because of the situation, which makes it less obvious that a leap is about to happen.

Your Baby's
10 Great Fussy Phases

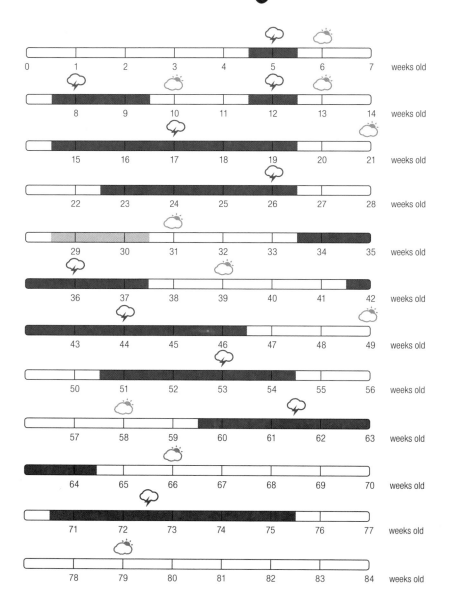

☐ Your baby is probably going through a comparatively uncomplicated phase

☐ Fussy and irritable behavior at around 29 or 30 weeks is not a telltale sign of another leap. Your baby has simply discovered that their mommy or daddy can walk away and leave them behind. Funny as it may sound, this is progress. It is a new skill: they are learning about distances.

■ Your baby may be fussier now than before.

⚡ Around this week, a "stormy" period is most likely to occur.

⛅ Around this week, it is most likely that your baby's sunny side will shine through

Do babies get sick more often during a leap?

Many babies don't get sick during the leap but do shortly after. This is because they have to process so many new things that they're prone to illnesses. Your baby doesn't sleep well during this difficult time, eats less, and doesn't feel well. These are the ingredients for getting sick. T. Berry Brazelton, a famous pediatrician, has observed that parents come to his office considerably more often after their child has taken a leap. However, illnesses should never be underestimated. If you are concerned about your baby's health, you need to see a pediatrician immediately. It's probably nothing, but it's better to be safe than sorry.

Why are some leaps more difficult than others for babies?

You'll notice that your baby acts clingier, whinier, and moodier during some leaps but less so during others. This may be connected to your baby finding the skills that come with these leaps especially interesting, or that your child wasn't feeling well when the leap started. Always keep in mind that it's perfectly normal if one leap is more difficult than another for your baby. This is no reason for concern. Try to figure out why your baby reacts more severely to a certain leap, and help your baby when they are having a hard time with a leap.

How can I help my baby get through a leap?

Your baby is the only one who can acquire and process a leap. You can't make it more comfortable for your baby, but you can certainly make it easier. You can do this by:

- ✓ Exposing your baby to situations that stimulate the new perceptual ability

- ✓ Making sure your baby gets well-deserved rest in time

One week before your baby takes a leap, read the chapter in *The Wonder Weeks* pertaining to the leap. That way, you'll know what your baby will soon be interested in, so you can prepare and offer everything they need. You're helping your baby process the impressions of the leap simply by enabling them to discover a new world. All the new impressions your baby receives during a leap take a lot of energy; therefore, your baby will need to rest. Sometimes just a short nap will do, but at other times your baby may want to sleep for a few hours. You are the one who can tell best when your baby needs rest. By making sure they rest in a timely manner, you make it easier for your baby to process a leap.

Do smart children do everything on the check off lists right after a leap?

As soon as your baby has completed a leap in mental development, they are able to do certain new things that they simply weren't able to do before. With the new cognitive ability, which was added with a leap, your child is now capable of learning a spectrum of new skills. The spectrum is so large and includes so many new things that there's no way for your child to do everything at the same time. Your baby acquired the new ability without asking for it because they are at the age when the brain makes the ability possible.

Without asking for it, your child is now able to do hundreds of new things, which doesn't mean that they will master them all at once. The saying "practice makes perfect" pertains to everything in life. Your baby will, try out a few things that are new all by themselves, which will be things that appeal to them. The starting point is a subconscious selection of some of the many skills. Your child will then practice, practice, and practice until the skills are mastered. At this point, your child will pick out something else from all the new options and start practicing it.

The number of new things your baby chooses after completing a leap doesn't reveal anything at all about intelligence, so don't consider the list with new possible skills that pertain to each leap to be a check-off list. Resist the urge of making this into a to-do list. No baby in the world is able to do everything at once. Be fair to yourself and to your baby. Look at the things your baby is fascinated with and what new things your baby wants to try out. That way, you cater to your baby, giving them self-confidence and a solid foundation for secure bonds (see also Chapter 6, "Emotional Development," page 105).

Are there leaps while a baby still in the womb as well as after the 10th leap?

Human beings take mental leaps their whole life, so they probably occur while still in the womb. Think of puberty and the midlife crisis, when you're right in the midst of them, you don't consider them to be fun, but they're ultimately defining periods in life. Our development never comes to a standstill.

CHAPTER 2

Physical Development

Gross Motor Skills, Fine Motor Skills,
Growth, and Reflexes

During the first years of a baby's life, mainly within the first 12 months, a lot happens but not only in a child's head; a baby discovers their body and learns to use it. Within a year and a half, the little one changes from a baby that's born with a number of reflexes to a toddler, who grabs things, crawls, or even walks. The child is getting bigger and increasingly stronger and is better able to use their body.

Is it true that children also go through physical growth spurts?

Every parent can tell you a thing or two about their child's clothes suddenly being too small. Children literally outgrow their clothes from one day to the next. The physical growth spurts and the mental leaps have something in common; they happen suddenly and unannounced. However, they don't happen at the same time.

Do the inherent reflexes babies are born with disappear during the leaps?

You probably know that there is a whole series of inherent reflexes. Reactions take place right after a baby's birth without the baby having to think about them. Some are tested by the midwife or doctor present at the delivery. What many people don't know is that the inherent reflexes vanish and are replaced by other reflexes! Vanishing reflexes and the development of new ones, however, don't happen in connection with a leap.

Does teething coincide with leaps?

The age at which babies start teething varies greatly per child. Teething, therefore, doesn't have anything to do with leaps in development.

Teething Doesn't Necessarily Happen During the Leaps!

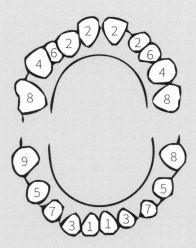

This image shows you the order in which teeth usually erupt. However, babies aren't machines. Your baby gets their first tooth when they are ready for it. It's a matter of disposition. How long it takes for the teeth to appear and how much time there is between the appearance of each tooth doesn't reveal anything about your baby's health or stage of development. Bright babies may get their teeth early or late, quickly or slowly.

In most cases, the first tooth breaks through the gum when babies are six months old. It generally starts with the two bottom front teeth (1). Usually, a child has six teeth by the time they celebrate their first birthday. At the age of two and a half years, the last molars (8) appear and complete the primary set of teeth. At that time, a toddler has 20 teeth.

Below, you can record the dates and sequence in which your baby's teeth appear.

Caution: diarrhea and/or fever don't have anything to do with teething. If your baby has these symptoms, it's usually a sign of sickness.

Date:

1.	11.
2.	12.
3.	13.
4.	14.
5.	15.
6.	16.
7.	17.
8.	18.
9.	19.
10.	20.

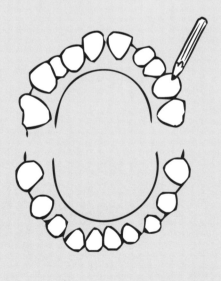

Does the head circumference also change during leaps?

There are indeed certain stages in life during which the head suddenly grows in circumference. This often happens before a leap in mental development. It happens for the first time approximately after three weeks, and then when your baby is seven or eight weeks, at 11 weeks, and at around 15 weeks. Anything beyond that hasn't been measured. Just as with the leaps in mental development, you have to use the calculated delivery date as the starting point, not the actual date of birth. A baby's brain doesn't grow any faster if the baby was born early and is not slower if they stay in your belly for 42 weeks.

What kind of physical developments are there, and why is this not the same in all babies?

Everything your baby does with their body falls under physical development and is divided into gross motor skills (holding up the head, turning around, sitting, grabbing, crawling, walking, running, etc.) and fine motor skills (reaching for something specific, holding a pen, pushing a button, doing a puzzle, etc.). If a child is more interested in gross motor skills, they will focus on mastering these skills quickly. A child who's more interested in fine motor skills will do everything it takes to learn all of the things in this category. What's noticeable is that children who mainly like observing are also often interested in fine motor skills, so don't only pay attention to the gross motor skills when studying your baby's physical development.

Which one is more important: fine motor skills or gross motor skills?

We need both in life; therefore, you can't say that one is more important than the other. The important thing is that you give your baby the opportunity to practice both. Play games that promote the gross motor skills and games where the focus is on the fine motor skills. However, always let your baby decide whether or not they want to play a game. Babies won't learn anything when they are forced to play a game they don't feel like playing. Even worse, they will develop a dislike towards the game.

Does the development of gross motor skills take place at the same age in all babies?

To many people, what counts first and foremost are clearly visible end results. That's why parents are often asked, "Is your child walking yet?" or "Is your child is crawling already?" All of these questions are completely redundant and may even upset you. Always keep in mind that a child only does something when they are ready to do it, and the point in time when a child is ready doesn't reveal anything about intelligence or development. Parents may find it comforting to know that the point in time that babies are able to sit, stand, crawl, or walk can vary greatly from one child to the next. It's also good to know the earliest point in time your baby will be able to perform a certain action. The earliest expected time children will be able to learn something new is determined by the leaps in mental development. Of course, children have to have the mental ability for a certain movement before being able to control their body.

Milestones in Gross Motor Skills

(A) Controlling the head when the shoulders are being held

Behavior	Average Age	Range of ages
Lifts the head	Neonatal period	
Corrects posture	Neonatal period	
Head upright-vertical	3 weeks	9 days to 3 months
Head upright-stable	7 weeks	3 weeks to 4 months
Holds head stable	2½ months	1 to 5 months
Head poised	4 months and 1 week	2 to 6 months

(B) Gross motor skills in abdominal position

Sideways head movements	Newborn	
Tiger crawl	2 weeks	Newborn to 3 months
Pushes themselves up with arms	Shortly after 2 months	3 weeks to 5 months
Able to move forward in one way or another	Shortly after 7 months	5 to 11 months

(C) Motor behaviors in supine position or on side

Playfully kicks with arms	3½ weeks	9 days to 2 months
Playfully kicks with legs	3½ weeks	9 days to 2 months
Holds on to a large plastic ring	3½ weeks	9 days to 2 months
Lifts head when the back of the head is resting on surface	1 month and 3 weeks	3 weeks to 4 months
Rolls from one side to the other	2 months	3 weeks to 5 months
Rolls from stomach to side	2½ months	2 to 7 months

Walking*, Keeping Balance, and Climbing Stairs

(A) Walking		
Behavior	Average Age	Range of ages
First steps	7 months and 2 weeks	5 to 11 months
Stepping movements	8 months and 3 weeks	6 to 12 months
Walks with assistance	9 ½+ months	7 to 12 months
Sits down	9 ½+ months	7 to 14 months
Stands on their own	11 months	9 to 16 months
Walks without assistance	11 months and 3 weeks	9 to 17 months

(B) Keeping balance		
Stands on right foot with assistance	16 months	12 to 21 months
Stands on left foot with assistance	16+ months	12 to 23 months
Stands on right foot without assistance	22 months and 3 weeks	15 to 30+ months
Stands on left foot without assistance	23 ½ months	16 to 30+ months
Jumps up and gets both feet off the floor	23 ½ months	17 to 30+ months

(C) Climbing stairs		
Climbs stairs with assistance	16+ months	12 to 23 months
Goes down stairs with assistance	Almost 16 ½ months	13 to 23 months
Climbs stairs without assistance, with both feet on each step	25+ months	18 to 30+ months
Goes down stairs without assistance, with both feet on each step	25 months and 3 weeks	19 to 30+ months
Climbs stairs without assistance, while alternating feet	30+ months	23 to 30+ months

* including motoric control when standing

Sitting and Standing

(A) Sat down by an adult		
Behavior	Average Age	Range of ages
Sits with support	2 months and 1 week	1 to 5 months
Sits with minimal support	3 months and 3 weeks	2 to 6 months
Briefly sits without assistance	5 months and 1 week	4 to 8 months
Sits without assistance for 30 seconds or longer	6 months	5 to 8 months
Sits stably without assistance	6 ½ months	5 to 9 months
Sits without assistance and is coordinated	7 months	5 to 10 months

(B) Sitting with the help of an adult		
Tries to sit down	4 months and 3 weeks	3 to 8 months
Pulls themselves up to a sitting position	5 months and 3 weeks	4 to 8 months
Pulls themselves up to a standing position	8 months	5 to 12 months

(C) Sitting/standing using furniture		
Sits up without help	8 months and 1 week	6 to 11 months
Gets up by their own efforts	8 ½ months	6 to 12 months
Stands up, level I	12 ½ months	9 to 18 months
Stands up, level II	22 months	11 to 30+ months
Stands up, level III	30+ months	22 to 30+ months

Source: Collaborative Perinatal Research Project of the Bayley Tests

Should I be worried if my baby doesn't learn something quickly in regards to gross motor skills?

The brain controls the body, so a baby's brain has to be capable of doing something before being able to control the body. In this book, we're describing at which point in time the brain is able to set the body in motion, which is the earliest expected time your baby will be capable of performing a certain action. This pertains to the development of the baby's gross motor skills as well as the fine motor skills. Whether a baby is going to do it or not depends on a variety of factors, including:

- ✓ How interested a baby is in the things they are able to do with the gross motor or the fine motor skills

- ✓ Whether the body is able to perform what the brain wants it to do

Why do some babies crawl and walk sooner than others?

Some babies are simply not interested in crawling or walking. Some babies are more interested in, for example, spatial aspects provided by stacking games and interlocking plastic bricks. This may engross their mind completely. These little ones won't try very hard when learning to walk either; they would rather do something else. They start crawling or walking once it's a resource for them

to achieve something else, such as when they absolutely want a specific building brick that they can't otherwise get to. Then, they try crawling to get to the object. Their goal is not the crawling itself but getting their hands on the brick.

Compare it to buying a car. Some people buy a pretty, luxurious car because they like driving it. Others aren't interested in what kind of car it is as long as it takes them from A to B.

Babies who are interested in gross motor skills will start crawling and walking considerably sooner than babies who aren't interested in those activities. It makes sense because you don't do anything you're not interested in. Those babies are going to try anything to learn a new acrobatic trick as soon as their mental development permits it. They practice and practice until they are able to stand, crawl, or walk. They enjoy the physical activity and are proud and beam with joy when they succeed.

One group of babies is not better or smarter than the other. It is very important that you, as parents, always react positively and actively to your baby's interests. Observe your child attentively and listen to what they are "telling" you whether with words or through body language. Never force your baby to do something they have absolutely no interest in.

How should I react when my baby wants to try out gross motor skills but simply doesn't have the physical ability yet?

Sometimes, babies would love to sit, walk, or crawl, but they realize their body doesn't obey. That results in frustration. The fact your baby is mentally capable of sitting, crawling, and walking and is also interested in these skills doesn't necessarily mean that your baby is actually able to do these things. You need your body for physical activity; however, sometimes, the body is not quite there, yet. The muscles aren't strong enough or the body is still too heavy for its limited muscular strength. It is very understandable that your baby gets frustrated when they want something, are excited about it, and feel the urge to do it but are unable to because they are stuck in a body that doesn't comply.

Support your baby in their efforts by praising them extensively. Encourage your baby, and assure them they're doing a really good job. You'll notice that your child's frustration will dwindle. Also, you can help your child manage the physical "trick" by playing exercising games, but always stop as soon as you realize that it's getting too much for your little one.

Can I help my baby to master physical skills?

Certainly, you can help, but don't force anything. The best way to help your child is to provide the opportunity and time needed to develop the skills. This holds true for all aspects of development.

Do the necessary exercises with your child, and make sure your child can practice what they need to master the new physical development. You, as parents, have to provide the general conditions. Sometimes, you simply have to lay your child in a certain position; at other times, you have to adjust something in your child's surroundings. The following table gives you an idea of what you should do.

What to practice	What to do
Training neck muscles	✓ Lay the baby on a soft blanket on their belly.
Learning to using the body	✓ Every once in a while, lay your baby down naked.
Learning grabbing	✓ Hold a toy in front of you child so they can grab it easily.
Sitting	✓ Put the nursing pillow around your baby.
Crawling	✓ Sit your baby on a floor that's not too slippery or hard.
Walking	✓ Hold your child by their hand, or give them some other kind of support. ✓ Let your child go barefoot, or put antiskid socks on their feet.

Why should you leave babies naked every now and then?

Clothes, no matter how soft they are, are still somewhat restrictive. Clothes also prevent your baby from feeling their body. It's no different for babies than it is for us. Your baby finds it wonderful to lie around naked without restrictions. Get in the habit of giving your child this wonderful feeling every day. Needless to say, your child shouldn't be lying in a draft or on a cold floor because babies are very sensitive to cold temperatures.

How do I see that it's getting too much for my baby?

If you pay careful attention to your baby's signals, you get to know their boundaries and when something is too much. You see it in your baby's sleepy eyes or in their body, which is suddenly getting limper. Sometimes, your baby's hints are so subtle that only you are able to read them correctly, unlike the neighbor who doesn't see your child every day. If your baby is playing with somebody and you notice that it's getting too much, you should interfere. Always make sure that your baby doesn't get overexerted when playing an exercising game.

Why is it so important to pay attention to the baby's neck?

The head is attached to the neck, and in babies, the head is relatively big compared to the body, much bigger than in adults. If adults still had the same proportions, our head would be almost as wide as our shoulders. So, on top of your baby's small neck is a huge and heavy body part. If you take in consideration that a baby's neck muscles are not as developed as those of an adult, it becomes obvious that it's hard work for your baby to lift their head and hold it upright. If your baby lifts their head and suddenly tilts it sideways, it can result in severe injuries. Don't ever underestimate this danger; always keep an eye on your baby's neck.

Below, you'll see the relation of human extremities throughout various stages of development. Do you see that the head of a baby is much larger in relation to the baby's legs compared to the body of an adult?

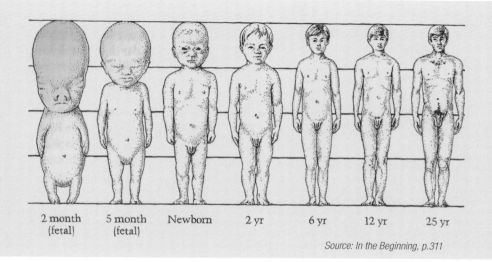

| 2 month (fetal) | 5 month (fetal) | Newborn | 2 yr | 6 yr | 12 yr | 25 yr |

Source: In the Beginning, p.311

Did you Know?

Between birth and adulthood:
✓ The head becomes twice as big
✓ The torso becomes three times as big
✓ The arms become four times as big
✓ The legs become five times as big

Can babies overdo their physical training?

Most babies stop on their own when an exercising game is getting too much for them. You can tell by looking at some babies, though, that they're going beyond their limits. Those little ones still have to learn to take a break when an exercise is getting too much. Your job as parents is to recognize your child's limits and protect your child from themselves. On the other hand, you also have to make sure to keep your own excitement at bay. You may find it exciting that your baby is sitting, turning, standing, crawling, or walking. However, if your child still has difficulty with the activity or is exhausted, you do more harm than good if you keep the game going. Don't ever force anything.

How come my child's body is limper after a leap in development?

Whenever your baby takes a leap, there's a brief step back in their development. Suddenly, your child isn't able to do things that they could do before the leap. Of course, this passes quickly, so there's no reason to worry. Your child's body may seem limper, but the muscles and bones aren't. Your child is just occupied with something else at the moment and briefly forgets how to use their body as they did before. A baby who's 18 weeks old and who was pretty good at holding their head upright is, for instance, not able to do this anymore during the leap at around 26 weeks. This is the reason for little accidents, such as falls, during or shortly after a leap. Keep this in mind and be extra careful during this time.

Can you say that a baby is "helping" when they lift their bottom when I am changing the diaper?

Once your baby has taken the leap into "smooth transitions" (about 12 weeks after the calculated delivery date), you'll notice that your baby pushes up their bottom when you are changing their diaper. Your child knows what's about to happen and beats you to it. As cute as this may seem and as handy as it is for you, it doesn't mean that your baby is trying to make it easier for you. Helping in order to please someone is a skill babies don't have until around the age of 55 weeks.

When is the best time to start "pulling-up games?"

Starting with the leap that takes place 12 weeks after the calculated delivery date, you may start playing "pulling-up games" if your baby has a desire and the physical capability to do so. Lay your child on their back in front of you, in your lap, or on a blanket on the floor. Take your child by the hands and stretch their little arms. That way, you basically invite your child to rise up to a sitting position. If your child tries to pull up, you may help a little bit. If your child doesn't make an effort to rise up, don't do anything. In this case, your child is simply not ready. Make sure to keep the baby's head from making nodding movements.

What should you do if a baby doesn't want to lie in the stroller but would rather look around?

Almost every stroller is equipped with a multi-position reclining seat, so a child can lie flat or sit up and admire the world. Starting at the age of six months, you can sit your child in the stroller. You'll notice that after the leap of "relationships" (26 weeks, or six months, after the calculated delivery date), your child is not content just lying in the stroller anymore. Your little one wants to look at everything while being pushed in the stroller, so choose a stroller with an adjustable seat and put it on the lowest setting. As long as your walk doesn't last too long, your baby can handle this position well and their brain is being fed by everything they see around them.

My baby always wants to sit when in the stroller. Isn't this too much for my child?

Some babies are so curious about their surroundings that they simply can't get enough even if this means torturing their little bodies in a seating position. A bouncer is ideal for these babies. Choose a bouncer that's adjustable, and pay attention to your baby's head when choosing a setting. If baby's head tilts sideways, you need to adjust the bouncer to a more reclined position. Adjust the bouncer regularly. Always keep an eye on your baby, and always pay attention to their head posture.

Why do some babies scoot backwards before really crawling forward?

Not all babies scoot backwards before learning how to crawl. As soon the leap into "events" has been taken, babies are capable of perceiving events, controlling them with their bodies, and learning skills such as crawling. Therefore, a baby could crawl if they desire to do so. However, it doesn't come easy to children just like all the other skills. The skills literally have to be learned by falling down and getting back up. And to do that, babies try everything they can. You get to see the craziest techniques, and scooting backwards is one of them. Most of the time, this doesn't last long. You'll see that, within a week, your baby will try all kinds of variations. Once your little one discovers how to really crawl, it'll go quickly, and at that point, your child will let go of the other variations. Even if a baby has mastered crawling, you'll still get to see funny mistakes. For example, one baby had a pretty good idea about crawling but was still clearly in doubt about which hand (left or right) and which knee (left or right) to move in which order. When the baby moved the right hand and the right knee at the same time, they fell over, of course. The result was angry screaming. Two days later, though, the baby was happily crawling around.

Why don't all babies crawl? And do babies miss out if they don't crawl?

Most babies crawl for a while before starting to walk. Others crawl for only a short period of time, and others skip crawling altogether. They may, for instance, scoot around in a sitting position or on their belly. Others only scoot backwards and turn around to move forward. There are some indications that it's good for a child's development to crawl in the classic way first before learning to walk. When crawling, a child sees the world from a different perspective, which benefits their sense of vision and space. Of course, you can't force your child to crawl. You can encourage your little one, though, by playing crawling games and by making the surroundings "crawl-friendly." A cold, hard floor that hurts the knees doesn't encourage crawling.

Do you have to put shoes on your child when they are learning to walk?

Shoes were invented to protect our feet from the cold, dirt, and anything that could hurt, but they don't promote walking. Quite the opposite, your baby learns to use their feet better when barefoot or when wearing antiskid socks, which is the best option for indoors. There are special slippers that cover their little feet and ensure that they don't get cold. If you have a cold floor, these are a good purchase. You don't need to buy shoes until your child is running around outside. And when you do, always choose good quality shoes. It's okay to watch the pennies when buying luxury items but not when it comes to shoes. The important thing is that the shoes provide good support, are soft, and offer enough room for your little one's feet to grow in them. At a good shoe store, you'll get advice and answers to your questions.

Is there a connection between the intelligence quotient and mastering the fine motor skills?

There is, in fact, a connection between the measurable IQ (also see Chapter 8, "Intelligence," page 133) and the fine motor skills. Although in little children IQ, EQ, or any other forms of intelligence cannot be measured through tests, it's proven that a higher or lower intelligence quotient at a later age coincides with a baby's fine motor skills. This relation was discovered when scientists did a Bayley test on a group of eight-month-old babies and observed their mental development, gross motor skills, and fine motor skills. Fine motor skills turned out to be the better indicator in estimating the IQ in a four-year-old child.

What is the process of developing the fine motor skill of "grabbing?"

Just as in the case of gross motor skills, you can't measure all babies by the same yardstick. Assuming a child is given the opportunity, they will start doing something when the time is right, not sooner or later. "Grabbing" is a skill your baby will start practicing soon. As soon as the leap of "events" has taken place at 19 weeks, children are able to move their hands in an attempt to grab something. Children learn to refine their grabbing technique at a later time. It calls for many months of practice for babies to master this skill. The following table (p. 55) shows you the development of "grabbing." You'll see the earliest expected point in time your baby should be able to perform a certain action and the average age babies master a certain aspects of grabbing.

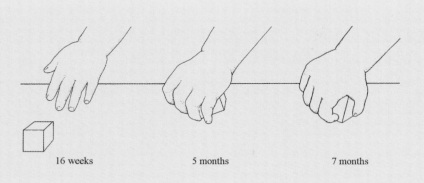

16 weeks   5 months   7 months

Do babies learn how to use their hands as soon as they've discovered them?

After the second leap at the age of eight weeks, your baby starts looking in amazement at the "things" that are attached to their arms. Your child twists and turns their hands, frowns, and twists them again. Your child sees that the hands are body parts but doesn't understand what to do with them until the third leap into "smooth transitions," which occurs 12 weeks after the calculated delivery date. At that time, you'll observe that your baby will try to grab something with their hands. It doesn't work all that well until the next leap. Once the next hurdle has been overcome, which is the leap of "events" occurring at 19 weeks after the calculated delivery date, your baby will be mentally capable of holding on to something but will still need your help.

Grabbing or Using the Hand While Sitting and Fine Motor Skills Involving the Hand

(A) Grabbing		
Performance	Average Age	Age range in months
Grabs cubes with outstretched elbow bone and palm (see p. 54)	3 months and 3 weeks	2 to 7 months
Grabs cubes, partially using the thumb (see middle drawing)	5 months	4 to 8 months
Grabs cubes using the thumb (see drawing on page 54)	7 months	5 to 9 months

(B) Manual dexterity		
Reaches for objects using one hand only	5 ½ months	4 to 8 months
Twists wrist	5 months and 3 weeks	4 to 8 months
Combines objects in front of them	8 ½ months	6 to 10 months
Plays clapping in front of them	9 months and 3 weeks	7 to 15 months

(C) Skills when using small balls		
Tries to grab	5 ½ months	4 to 8 months
Moves hands like shovels	6 months and 3 weeks	5 to 9 months
Grabs, partially with fingers (incomplete pinch grip)	7 months and 2 weeks	6 to 10 months
Grabs precisely (complete pinch grip)	9 months	7 to 10 months

Source: In the Beginning, p. 320

Why does my baby kick or hit toys?

Kicking or hitting toys announces grabbing. Your baby clearly shows interest in the toy and tries to get to the object of interest using their whole body but doesn't quite succeed yet. During this phase, a baby gym is a great thing to have, especially since your baby can achieve something just by hitting or kicking an object. The toys are attached and move up and down when a child touches them, so the child's efforts are rewarded!

What can I do to help my baby with learn how to grab?

Whenever you notice that your baby wants to get a hold of something, hold the object of interest at a distance that your baby can easily reach. By observing carefully, you'll find out to what extent your child can manage the process of grabbing through their own efforts. You can help your child complete the process by, for example, turning the toy to a position where it fits better in their little hands. You'll realize that, over time, you'll have to help less and less.

Why do babies take everything apart and throw everything on the floor?

When we think of playing with building bricks, we mainly think of building a nice tower or stacking bricks. Babies don't understand the concept of "creating" until they have accomplished the leap of "programs." Before that, children experiment with the individual parts and what they can do with them. That's why it's so fascinating for a child to knock over the tower you just built, to see everything fall down with a big racket, and to watch you skid across the floor collecting the pieces. There is a great fascination with falling objects because it goes right along with the leap of "events" at 19 weeks. The excitement over falling bricks is not destructive behavior, and it also doesn't mean that there's something wrong with your baby's fine motor skills, which are necessary to neatly stack bricks. As soon as your baby has accomplished the leap of "programs," they will enthusiastically build things and stack building bricks, which is good practice for fine motor skills. Your baby will then learn to move their hands in a way to put one brick on top of another.

Which toys are good for practicing fine motor skills?

Basically, all toys with knobs or holes are suitable to practice fine motor skills. Puzzles, little bricks, or an activity center are ideal. However, toys aren't the only qualifying purchase; your child is also fascinated with household items. Give your little one a cup and a spoon to stir with, or ask your child to turn the pages of a book. Fine motor skills are so integrated in our everyday life that they can be practiced anywhere as long as it's fun. The main thing is *how* you practice them with your baby, not what you use to practice with.

It's very important for you to demonstrate the movements clearly and calmly. For adults, it's nothing special to push a button, but it is hard work for your baby; your little one has to understand to use *one* finger instead of the whole hand and that the finger has to be moved precisely. If you demonstrate correctly, you will increase the speed and precision with which your child learns to master the skill. Always demonstrate everything in a way that shows your baby exactly what's going on and how you use your hand. Praise your child's efforts even when they're not successful. Keep encouraging your child.

Keep in mind that the toy your baby plays with should not be too difficult for them to handle. For instance, try out the buttons of a toy before purchasing it. Some buttons are tight and hard to push. If that's the case, choose a different one with buttons that can be operated easily. Some toys that are made for babies are not always appropriate to their level of development.

CHAPTER 3

Sleep

Rest, Deep Sleep, Sleep Patterns,
Dreaming, and Processing

Your baby grows a lot mentally and physically in the first year. They need a lot of sleep. But sleep can be difficult. As a parent, you spend nights wandering between your own bed and your baby's hoping that tonight you can close your eyes for a few hours. But now for the good news: there's good reason your baby has a different sleep pattern. Those short naps, waking up, the 'crazy' rhythm... they're all part of healthy development!

What are sleep problems?

Let's cut to the chase: your baby has no problems with the way they sleep. It's us, the adults, who see it as a problem. There's a reason why a baby sleeps more lightly, for shorter periods and wakes more often than we do. They then make a noise indicating that they want to see and feel you again. Their sleep rhythm and sleep cycle are very different from ours. And since we need that long night of sleep to function well 'problems' occur. Problems for us adults – not for the baby! That's reassuring, but then again it isn't. You will notice that when you understand the sleep-wake rhythm and your baby's sleep cycle, you will find it easier to reach a solution to (your) sleep problems that suits your family, circumstances, and lifestyle.

What is a sleep-wake rhythm?

The sleep-wake rhythm is one of the many day and night rhythms we know as humans. Your body's biological clock adapts to the earth's light-dark cycle. For example, you produce less urine at night than during the day. Also, your heartbeat slows and your body temperature lowers. You (fortunately!) produce less stress hormones and more melatonin during the night. Melatonin is the sleep hormone that ensures you relax and stay asleep. All these things are examples of the various day and night rhythms we have. The sleep-wake rhythm is only one of those. Without these different day and night rhythms we adults cannot sleep as we do. And that's just it... your newborn baby doesn't have these day and night rhythms yet. They can't yet sleep like we do!

Sleep-wake chart. But how do I interpret these?

The graph on page 63 beautifully illustrates how babies sleep. Black represents sleep, white awake. In the first weeks, you see only chaos. Your baby's sleeping and waking is scattered throughout the day and night. That is logical now you know the biological processes for a sleep-wake pattern are simply not there.

It then becomes obvious between the sixth and fourteenth week that the waking periods seem to shift a little. If you look at this more precisely, you'll see that babies of that age live more to a 25-hour clock than a 24-hour one! This is logical too when you know that your baby's biological clock is not yet complete. This chart also shows that babies around 15 weeks follow a more stable sleep pattern. From that moment on you can fairly accurately assess when your baby will sleep.

An even more important conclusion can be drawn from the small white spots in the black strips that emerge from 15 weeks. The white strips represent being 'awake'. So it's normal for a baby to wake up regularly at night! Even if it's only for a short time, your baby is awake. It's not a problem for them as your baby simply falls straight back to sleep. But it is different for you. Those small white dots are a reflection of the sleep problems we experience when we have a baby. Those few minutes awake – when out of bed being fed and/or having their diaper changed – are very normal for your baby, but very hard for us.

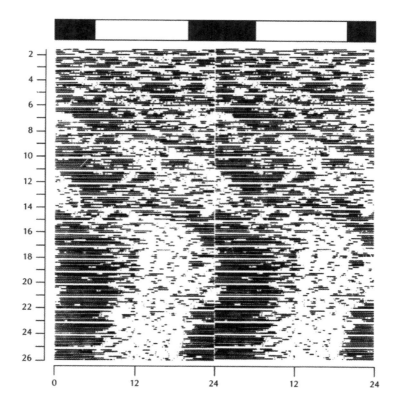

Source: Eibl-Eibesfeldt, I. (1989). Human Ethology. Hawthorne, New-York: Aldine de Gruyter. p. 73, figure 2.49. Originally published in Kleitman, N., & Engelmann, T. G. (1953). Sleep characteristics of infants. Journal of Applied Physiology, 6(5), 269.

Nice to Know:

Newborn baby: has no day and night rhythms at all, making the sleep-wake rhythm chaotic.

Birth to 6 days: Your baby spreads their naps over the 24 hours of the day. You will not see a differeance in the hours or times they sleep during the day or the night.

1 week: The day and night rhythm of your baby's body temperature emerges. To achieve a good sleep-wake rhythm, your baby first needs this day and night body temperature rhythm. You could consider the day and night body temperature rhythm as a gauge of the emergence and development of a sleep-wake pattern.

6 weeks: Your baby now has the foundations of a waking rhythm. Not a sleep rhythm yet! The waking rhythm develops earlier than the sleeping rhythm!

Two months: Your baby now begins developing the very first precursors of a sleep-wake pattern. You won't notice that immediately, but it is nice to know that, biologically, the night rhythm has started in the developmental process!

3 months: The time your baby sleeps during the day decreases and the time your baby sleeps at night increases.

(3-6 months): A pattern increasingly develops in the nocturnal melatonin production. From now on there is also a measurable difference in cortisol levels between night and day.

Babies sleep through the night... a myth?

In the first months, 95 percent of babies cry when they wake up during the night and need their mom or dad. From eight months, 60 to 70 percent of babies can get themselves back to sleep. Most parents think that their six-month-old baby sleeps through the night. Many development specialists see 'sleeping through' as a notable milestone. However, that's incorrect. Research with a hidden camera shows that babies do wake up, but that they fall back asleep without crying. Virtually no children under twelve months of age sleep through the night without interruption. All children wake up one to three times. Waking usually starts after four hours' sleep.

What is a sleep cycle?

A sleep cycle consists of Non-REM sleep followed by REM sleep. REM stands for 'Rapid Eye Movement'. The eyes move back and forth behind the closed eyelids. Broadly speaking, you could say that the Non-REM sleep is the inactive, deep sleep and the REM sleep the active, light sleep. During Non-REM sleep you relax and during REM sleep you process things. This is a simplification, but in essence that's what occurs. As adults we spend most of the time in Non-REM sleep, the deep sleep. A baby... in REM sleep. That's why babies sleep lighter than we do and to us that seems restless. A few sleep cycles occur every night. We can wake up between sleep cycles and then enter the following sleep cycle, or we can go immediately from one sleep cycle to the next without waking up. Babies usually wake up between sleep cycles. Another big difference between our sleep cycle and our baby's is the length. Our sleep cycle lasts a lot longer than that of a baby. So your baby wakes up more frequently.

Why do babies spend more time in REM sleep?

Research increasingly shows that the blood supply to the brain almost doubles during REM sleep. Everything points towards the fact that during this part of sleep there is extra brain stimulation and many brain connections are created. Therefore, REM sleep is incredibly important for your baby's mental development.

Is enough sleep important for a baby's mental development?

Learning and discovering many things asks a lot of your baby's body and brain. The brain, where mental development takes place, is a part of their body too. Besides food, the body also needs rest. When your baby gets enough sleep, they will learn and discover new things more easily than if they are tired.

How do I know that my baby is getting enough sleep?

People differ and we all need different amounts of sleep. It depends on the time our brain and nervous system need to rest. That also applies to your baby, infant and toddler. Naturally there are averages. A baby in the womb sleeps on average 23 out of 24 hours. Shortly after birth the average baby sleeps 16 hours a day. The length of sleep varies from 10 to 23 hours! You may wonder if those averages are important to know as they don't say anything about your baby! Although we've given you some averages here, don't place too much emphasis on them. Let your baby direct their own unique sleep needs.

Why do some babies sleep less during a leap?

Your baby's world suddenly changes completely when they make a leap. They haven't asked for it and have no influence on it, but suddenly everything looks different. They get upset and you notice it in their sleep pattern. Every baby reacts differently to a leap. One baby hardly sleeps, another sleeps less at night and more during the day, and yet another doesn't manage to fall asleep despite trying. By far the majority of babies sleep less and are more 'restless' during a leap. But there are also babies who simply sleep during a leap like they normally do. Unfortunately, these are few and far between. If you know when your child is experiencing a leap, it's easier to cope with any sleep difficulties. You know it's just part of it all and that's reassuring.

Is there anything I can do to help my baby sleep well during a leap?

Unfortunately, you can't get your baby to sleep with a magic formula. If only that were possible! You can help by giving them the chance to process all the new impressions of that leap. Take it a bit easier on the days your baby makes a leap. Delay things and take the pressure off them for a few days. Maybe this means a bit of diary shuffling, but in the long run your baby – and you – will benefit from the rest.

How can I avoid not getting enough sleep myself and from being too exhausted to be a good parent on the leap days?

If your baby does not sleep you will start to feel the consequences of a lack of deep sleep. Some are more sensitive to this than others. If you notice you are so tired during the day that you almost take it out on your baby, you need to get your rest one way or the other. Leave the chores be and catch an hour's sleep during the day when your baby sleeps. Or ask your partner to look after your baby one night if your baby wakes up. You could express milk in the evening if you are breastfeeding.

Is the danger of suffocating over once a baby is able to turn on their side and push up when lying on their stomach?

In the Netherlands, we advise making the bed 'short' to prevent the baby from ending up with their face under the blankets and suffocating. That danger appears to diminish when a baby can roll over or move well. But that is only an illusion. If your child can roll over a few times or move well during the day that doesn't mean they can do that at night on a mattress as well. Play it safe and continue to make the bed 'short'.

Why does my baby always sleep when we have company or when we're visiting?

Some babies do not like large groups of people. They close their eyes and fall asleep or unconsciously 'play' that they are sleeping. Many parents find this frustrating. They want to show off that lovely smile and those gorgeous eyes to their friends. Yet it is not smart to wake your baby when they would rather sleep. You will notice that as your baby grows, they will like socializing more and then everyone can see how fantastic he or she looks.

Sometimes my baby briefly falls asleep when playing – is this normal?

Your baby is especially interested in new things. Anything new your baby can do or learn after a leap is very exciting. So exciting that they are fully absorbed in it, which takes a lot of energy. If playing becomes too much, your baby will often turn their head away. That is a sign for you that they want a moment of rest. After a short break, your child will continue. This goes on for a while until you see their eyes turn away. The tiredness takes over, turning into a short nap where your baby processes what they just experienced.

Is there a difference between boy and girls' sleeping patterns?

Research shows that boys up to six months need more sleep than girls. From six months onwards this reverses with girls needing more sleep than boys. And it remains that way. In older children, girls can usually recount their dreams better than boys. But they both dream just as frequently.

Do I have to be completely quiet when my newborn is asleep?

You don't have to be extra quiet when your baby is sleeping. A child has already heard all the ordinary household noises in the womb and has become used to them. If you are especially quiet, your child might perceive they are missing something and stay awake or wake up. Making extra noise is not necessary either. Just do what you usually do.

Do babies dream?

It still remains a mystery what dreaming actually is and why we dream. We do know in which phase of sleep humans dream. That's not in the deep sleep, but in the dream sleep, the REM sleep. REM stands for 'Rapid Eye Movement'. This sleep phase is called that because the eyes move very quickly. And precisely because a young baby has longer periods of dream sleep than we do, it seems logical that babies dream more than we do. It is hard to say if that really is the case and if their dreams can be compared to ours. Sometimes, as a parent, you can only see that your baby has had a good or a bad dream. But no-one knows if they dream 'stories' too or if they dream about basic feelings and emotions.

Do babies have nightmares?

Starting from the "relationship" leap (26 weeks or six months) many parents notice their baby sleeps restlessly and moves a lot during sleep, which makes it look as if the baby is having a nightmare. Some parents already notice this at four months. Nightmares can – just as in adults – occur at all times, but happen most frequently when we are stressed. Taking this into consideration, your baby may have more nightmares when going through a leap.

Should I wake my baby when it seems like they are having a nightmare?

You will notice that your baby wakes up by themselves when a dream becomes too much. You don't have to wake your baby up. But do comfort your child intensively if they wake. A nightmare is even worse for a baby than for us. When we wake up from a nightmare, we know how to reassure ourselves and understand it was only a dream. Your baby doesn't have that power yet. They really need someone close to offer comfort.

My baby is too active to go to sleep, especially after a leap. How can I help my baby get to sleep?

Some babies are naturally driven to achieve things and will not rest until they succeed. You can see this behavior from a very young age. Those babies do not allow themselves to sleep before they reach their goal. They demand a lot of themselves, and you. In itself, this is a personality trait that will be useful later in life, but at a young age you may need to protect these children from themselves. Place the emphasis on trying. Praise them for their attempts, irrespective of the end result. That way you distract your baby. If you notice your child is demanding too much of themselves, put a stop to the activity. Remove your baby from the challenging environment for a while and bring them into contact with something calmer. For example, read a book together.

Are there guidelines for sleep rituals?

You can do whatever you want to make your own sleep ritual cozy and relaxed. Everything is allowed, as long as it is quiet and you allow your baby to feel that tranquility. You can do things like reading a book, bathing and/or rocking your baby. Agree with your partner what you will do each night so you both apply the same ritual. Adults may consider such a strict pattern very boring, but your baby relies on it. It helps them to understand the situation. Make sure you are relaxed too when you put your baby to bed. A child is far more sensitive than an adult. They feel when you are stressed or in a hurry. So take the time to lay your baby in bed. The calm you exude will ensure that your baby falls asleep quickly and sleeps well. Of course, it only makes sense to set a sleep ritual if your baby has a good night rhythm.

Is it wise to give a baby a cuddly toy in bed?

A stuffed toy is cozy, nice and gives your child something to cuddle. There is nothing wrong with it. Don't force it though. Don't insist on a cuddly toy when your little one goes to bed just because it's cute. By doing that you give them the message that it's impossible to sleep without teddy and that's not the right message. Give your child a cuddly toy only if they ask for one. If your child doesn't ask for it, don't give it!

Do babies grow physically and mentally when sleeping?

As a parent, you sometimes think that your baby has grown in their sleep. That is somewhat true, although that growth can't be measured. When you sleep, the pituitary gland, the part of the brain that stimulates hormone production, produces the growth hormone. That growth hormone assures body growth.

Why is my baby suddenly scared when I leave the room when this was not the case before?

In the relationship leap, around six months, your baby suddenly understands that you can go away and that they are not with you. They understand that this situation (lying in bed) means you will not be there for a long time. Your baby gets upset and shows it; they don't want you to leave whereas that wasn't a problem before. That new fear is generated by the new understanding they have gained in that leap. Show your child that you understand. Just sit with them for a while or sit at the other end of the room where they can still see you. By respecting your child's fears and showing that you are there for them, their fears will subside quicker.

CHAPTER 4

Crying

Calming Down, Comforting, Processing,
and Communicating

All parents would prefer their baby to be laughing and happy all day long, but unfortunately, this is not always the case. Every baby cries, and all bewildered parents ask themselves why. They would like to comfort their baby and search for the right way to do this. Once parents have tried all kinds of things and baby has finally quietened down, they sigh in relief. It's all part of it.

Why do babies cry?

Your baby has only a few options to express themselves. The younger the baby, the more limited the options are. With every leap in development a child accomplishes, their verbal and nonverbal communication with you improves. Until your child is able to really tell you what's wrong, your only option is to use their crying and body language as a guide. A crying baby is not sad, but crying signals that your child is not feeling good for some reason.

The most common reasons for crying are:

- ✓ Sickness or pain
- ✓ A mental leap
- ✓ Hunger
- ✓ Frustration
- ✓ Boredom
- ✓ Lack of rest, cleanliness, or steadiness
- ✓ Processing the day

How do you know why your baby is crying?

As parents, you quickly get to know your baby's various crying sounds. After only a few weeks together, you know what your baby wants when they cry a certain way. However, sometimes your baby has a screaming fit that drives you to desperation because it hurts you to listen to your baby crying when you really can't figure out the reason for it.

In this case, check the following:

✓ Is your child sick (does your child have a fever), or could they possibly be in pain? Pain is sometimes difficult to determine, especially in very young babies. Signals are overly stretching the body to one side or overly tightening or stretching certain muscles. Babies demonstrate they have pain due to intestinal cramps, for instance, by extreme stretching or pumping of the legs.

✓ Whenever your baby takes a leap in mental development, your baby's world is turned upside down for quite a while. Your little one is confused, so it's no wonder they cry for longer periods of time during those days. Your baby may also cry differently than normal. Luckily, you can calculate the time of a leap; thus, you can easily figure out whether the crying is related to a leap.

✓ A baby's digestive system is completely different from ours, especially when a baby is still very little. Breast milk, for instance, is so easily digested that a baby is soon hungry again. This is one of the reasons that feeding on demand is much better than feeding according to a strict schedule. If a baby cries because of hunger, putting the baby to your breast quickly solves the problem. Formula is not as easily digested; therefore, babies are not hungry again soon after having a bottle. Satisfying your baby's hunger isn't difficult unless your baby doesn't suck hard enough when being breastfed or doesn't drink well when given a bottle (also see Chapter 5, "Diet," page 91).

✓ Sometimes a little baby is simply frustrated. It's a misapprehension to think that frustration requires an adult form of awareness. Frustration means that there are conflicting interests or processes in the brain causing the feeling of restlessness and tension. Your baby may indeed be frustrated because of not being able to get something across to you and because your baby doesn't know the reason behind his feeling. You can help alleviate your child's frustration through careful observation. Figure out what your baby likes and is interested in, and use it as a distraction. Since every baby is different, there are no hard and fast rules, but the more time you spend with your baby, the easier it gets. Interaction is even more important than time. The more you devote yourself to your child, the better you get to know them. If you sit for hours at a time next to your child's bed without saying or doing anything, you don't get to know your baby and you won't be able to find out the cause of their frustration or how to distract your baby.

✓ A baby can also be bored, no matter how young they are. There are extremely demanding babies and less demanding babies. The word "demanding" has a negative ring to it, but demanding babies usually have a distinct character and want to see, experience, hear, and feel lots of things.

That's why a demanding baby requires more energy and effort from you than a less demanding baby. If you give your child stimulation, opportunities for experiences, and adequate attention, you'll notice this reduces your child 's boredom and crying.

In the past, babies were raised on the basis of rest, cleanliness, and steadiness. Nowadays, we know that we shouldn't hold on to these rules too tightly. Exaggerated cleanliness, for example, isn't good for a child because coming into contact with everyday bacteria boosts the immune system. But there's also some truth in these old rules. A baby is bothered by a dirty diaper and cries because of it. The other two rules, rest and steadiness, should not be completely neglected either. During the first year, your child learns, grows, and experiences more than during any year thereafter. Your child takes in all the new impressions and is in dire need of rest. By providing a certain steadiness, you help your child deal with the various impressions. Your little one experiences enough chaos already, so don't make it any worse. Create order by integrating routine throughout the day. This order brings calmness. Routine is important, not just for babies but for all of us. During all the phases of development your child goes through, routine has a positive effect against whining and screaming fits, which you'll experience, there's no doubt about that (also see Chapter 9, "Parenting," page 149).

When is it baby colic?

If a baby cries more than three hours a day and more than three days a week over a period of more than three weeks, it's called baby colic. Baby colic is an enormous burden for parents. In order to find out whether you have a baby with colic, use the table below as an aid. Write down how many hours and minutes your baby cries each part of the day and how long they sleep. You may come to the conclusion that it just feels as if your baby is crying for hours, but once you really track the time and complete the table it's actually not as bad as you thought. This happens a lot. Crying is not fun for a child or for the parents, and that's why time seems to drag on. If you've filled out the table for a week and your baby actually comes close to the number hours of crying that could indicate a colicky baby, fill out the table for the following two weeks as well. If the crying behavior continues to the point your baby is really colicky, contact your pediatrician or a consultation center.

What is a "witching hour?"

A "witching hour" is the result of the maturation of the child's nervous system. The maturation enables the children to trade a short nap for longer periods of sleep. The maturation takes place in leaps, but these are not the same leaps as the leaps in mental development. Babies take the first maturation leap at the age of around three to four weeks. Babies do not sleep for three hours at a time until the age of 12 weeks, though. If the change in the sleep pattern causes your baby problems, it will result in a "witching hour."

Monday	Night	Morning	Afternoon	Evening
Sleeps				
Is awake				
- Cries				
- Screams				

Tuesday	Night	Morning	Afternoon	Evening
Sleeps				
Is awake				
- Cries				
- Screams				

Wednesday	Night	Morning	Afternoon	Evening
Sleeps				
Is awake				
- Cries				
- Screams				

Thursday	Night	Morning	Afternoon	Evening
Sleeps				
Is awake				
- Cries				
- Screams				

Friday	Night	Morning	Afternoon	Evening
Sleeps				
Is awake				
- Cries				
- Screams				

Saturday	Night	Morning	Afternoon	Evening
Sleeps				
Is awake				
- Cries				
- Screams				

Sunday	Night	Morning	Afternoon	Evening
Sleeps				
Is awake				
- Cries				
- Screams				

Does a "witching hour" mean the baby is sad?

The transition to a new sleep pattern is difficult (see Chapter 3, "Sleep," page 59). Children don't get over it until the age of 12 weeks. The baby's nervous system is still maturing. Until the nervous system matures, both deep sleep and light sleep aren't very effective. What goes wrong? During light sleep, you process what you've experienced during the day. Babies, too, do this in their own way. However, until your baby has settled into the new rhythm, they are unable to process everything that needs to be processed, and that's the problem. During the first nap of the day, your baby processes a lot, but there's still some information that's left unprocessed. The same happens the next time your baby sleeps and the time thereafter. At the end of the day, lots of unprocessed experiences have accumulated. At the same time, sleep and wake periods become shorter throughout the day. Everything gets thrown out of balance, and then comes the explosion: the "witching hour." As crazy as it may sound, the "witching hour" is liberating for your baby. It's Mother Nature's medicine to rebalance. By venting, your baby is finally able to process the accumulated impressions and emotions of the day. Now, the little one is ready for the next 24 hours.

When are "witching hours" most likely to occur?

Many little ones and their parents experience a daily "witching hour" between three and 12 weeks after birth. They're most common when babies are six weeks old. Often, parents are able to predict when it's about to happen because 85 percent of all babies are restless before it starts. The restlessness is an unmistakable signal for what's about to come. Usually, the crying stops after an hour or two, but sometimes, it may last four or even six hours. Luckily, there's some good news; once you've made it through the periods of crying, a baby usually sleeps longer and better and is better rested when awake.

What's the best way to comfort my crying baby?

Unfortunately, there are no tips on how to comfort with guaranteed success. It's usually the "classics" that work well. Your baby mainly wants rhythm, warmth, and safety. Walk around the room while rocking your baby in your arms, sing or hum a song. Look at your child with a calm expression and try to have a very peaceful look on your face, so your serenity will radiate to your child. The same applies to your voice. Say comforting words and use a soothing tone. Comfort your baby by saying that you understand and that you're there for them. Your baby doesn't understand the words and their exact meaning but feels the intention and is comforted.

Is it possible that my reaction to my baby's crying makes my baby even more troubled?

Babies are very sensitive to what their parents feel and radiate. If your baby cries and you react annoyed, their crying will become even louder. Before you know it, it becomes a downward spiral, and the crying lasts longer and longer. If you find yourself in such a situation, you have to come to your senses. Forget everything around you for just a moment. Pay close attention to your aura. Breathe deeply and calmly, and let your child feel your calm breathing by laying your child on your belly. Your baby feels your belly going up and down in a rhythmic motion and calms down, too.

Sometimes, parents are unable to keep calm no matter how hard they try because their child's crying is too penetrating and lasts so long. They admit they just can't take it any longer and can't bear to listen to their baby's screaming any more. Don't feel guilty; we're all human, and everybody has their limits. Never give up too quickly, but don't push your limits, either. If the crying really starts to become too much, put your baby in bed for a little while and leave the room. That way, you avoid a fierce reaction to your baby's crying, which has more negative consequences than your baby being alone for a short time.

At what point do I need to seek help when my baby cries a lot?

When it doubt, it's recommended that you contact a consultation center or the pediatrician, if only to relieve your concerns. They may refer you to other aid organizations. Of course, this only happens if the situation calls for it.

Why do some babies quieten down with certain music?

Tests have shown that babies like music that sounds warm, full, round, and soft. When the rhythm of the music is slower than their heartbeat, babies calm down. Classical music works especially well. There are also special songs that are composed in such a way that their sounds have a soothing effect on babies.

Why is physical contact so important when comforting a baby?

You are the one challenging your baby to get to know the world, and you are the one who gives your baby the feeling of emotional security while they explore the world. When you're close by, your baby feels safe. When your baby feels you, the feeling of emotional security is even stronger. Your baby gets calmer and relaxes physically as well as mentally. It may be very difficult for you to hold your baby while they are screaming, but a feeling of helplessness makes the penetrating sound even worse. Try to stay calm and in physical contact with your child anyway. Don't forget that the situation is harder on your child than it is on you.

Does bodily contact help calm a newborn?

Basically, all babies love bodily contact. Some babies just show it more than others. Your newborn loves to feel you close by. The warmth of your body, your heartbeat, and your voice remind your little one of the time in your womb. By the way, since your baby also knows Dad's voice from that time, your baby will enjoy his attention as well. A baby sling is ideal for babies who like constant intimate contact. When using a sling, you always have your baby close to you, but at the same time, you have your hands free for other things. You may choose fabric that you can wrap around you or purchase a special sling. You can also use the sling as a hammock in the playpen. Go to a specialty shop for baby items and try out the various slings. Choose the sling that is comfortable and suits you the best.

Is it normal that my baby calms down when lying on my naked body?

There's still kind of a taboo when it comes to nakedness. However, there's no reason to be embarrassed. Your baby loves to feel your naked skin against their body. That's why many babies get very calm when lying on their dad's or mom's naked belly for a little while. They become so calm they often fall asleep. When on your belly, your baby may fall asleep in the abdominal position. Always be considerate of safety when your baby's lying on your belly. For instance, never drink a hot drink, and never lay your baby naked on your belly when there's a draft.

Is massaging a baby a good way to comfort them?

A baby massage is ideal for relaxing your child, and during a gentle massage, your baby becomes aware of their body. Therefore, a baby massage is far more than simply for comfort and encouraging relaxation. A baby that is uncomfortable for whatever reason will benefit a lot from a relaxing massage.

When can I start massaging my baby?

You can start massaging your baby as early as five weeks. Some experts say that it's okay from the fourth week on. Make sure that you don't massage your baby right after feeding; it's better to wait half an hour. Also, consider your baby's general mood. If your baby is very tired, it's better to wait until after they have had a nap. Generally, the ideal time for a massage is right before bath time in the evening. During the bath, you can remove the massage oil with soap. Be careful when holding your child since your baby will be slippery from the oil!

At what age do tears appear when babies cry?

Your newborn doesn't cry tears yet. The first tears are not produced until babies are about four months old.

Baby Massage

1. Apply a little baby oil to your hands. Put your hands next to each other with your palms down so that both thumbs are in the middle of your baby's chest. Using the palm of your hand, rub gently from the middle of the chest outwards. Repeat five times.

2. Then move on to the arms. Take one of your baby's arms, close to the armpit, in both your hands. Then massage one arm, working your way towards your child's hand. Once your first hand is almost at your baby's hand, glide your other hand towards your baby's other hand. When your second hand is almost at the baby's hand, put your first hand close to the baby's armpit again. It may sound complicated, but it's not. If you do it right, you'll see that one hand is always massaging and that there is no interruption in the gentle rubbing motion.

3. You basically perform the same step again, but instead of a rubbing motion that goes straight to the baby's hand, make a spiraling motion.

4. Hold your baby's hand in your hand, and using your thumb, massage your baby's palm. If you see that your baby really likes this, you may also massage their little fingers. Don't force anything, though. If your baby tightens their fist so that you can't open it, skip this step.

5. Repeat steps 2, 3, and 4 on the other arm. Make sure to keep touching your baby's body with your hands when you switch over to the other arm. Massage with your fingers from one armpit across the chest to the other armpit.

6. Now, move your fingers across the chest and belly to the legs. You do basically the same here as you did with the arms. Again, make sure you keep touching the baby when switching from one leg to the other.

7. Now, it's the feet's turn! Press one thumb on your baby's heel and the other just in front of the toes and perform an up and down motion. Once your baby's a little older, they will start giggling.

8. Move back to the belly while continually touching your baby with your hands. Using the palm of your hands, make circles that gradually get smaller the closer you get towards the bellybutton.

9. Turn your baby on their stomach and perform long movements with your hands, starting at the neck and going across the back and down to their little feet.

The best thing to do is to make it a habit of massaging your baby regularly, not only when they are going through a difficult time, because they love it!

CHAPTER 5

Diet

Food Intake, Eating Behavior,
Eating and Drinking Problems,
and the Effects of Diet

You need energy to keep your body functioning. Your brain is, incidentally, the most energy – gulping organ! When your little one is two years old, they have more connections in the brain than at any point in their life, and a child's brain consumes twice as much energy as an adult's brain! The need for nutrition seems purely physical, but it's part of mental development, too. If your baby does not feel well, they do not eat well, and if you breastfeed your baby, they don't only drink milk but also love it. If your toddler wants to become independent, they refuse your help holding a spoon. Nutrition is more than just taking in nutrients; it is a social event, a happening where the body and mind work together intensively.

Do I have to write down what my baby takes in every day?

As long as your baby is growing well, you can assume that your child is taking in enough nutrients. Within the first few days, it's important to check your newborn drinks well, so during this phase, you need to observe your little one extra carefully. When you leave the hospital after delivery, the pediatrician or clinic is in charge of continuing care. Your baby gets weighed, and you can monitor whether your child is growing accordingly. Unlike during your stay in the hospital, your child is not measured daily. It's no longer necessary. From this point on, measurements are based on whether your baby is growing as it should over a period of a few weeks, which also shows whether or not your baby has taken in enough nourishment.

Do I have a reason to worry if my baby suddenly eats or drinks less?

Every now and then, your baby will have days when they drink less than usual. The smaller your baby is, the more you have to watch their drinking habits. When in doubt, you should visit a clinic or your pediatrician. Usually, it will probably be a false alarm, but it'll ease your mind. It's perfectly normal that babies drink or eat less when they are not feeling well. You are not as hungry when you don't feel well, either. Your baby may start eating or drinking less shortly before they get sick. You'll also notice that eating behavior changes during a leap in mental development; your baby will most likely eat less than usual. This is part of a leap and no reason for concern. Whenever you have doubts about your child's drinking or eating habits, ask your pediatrician.

My baby wants to be fed all the time when taking a leap in development. Does my baby need to drink more during that time?

Fortunately, we now know that it's better to breastfeed on demand, meaning you feed your baby when they want to be fed. After all, your baby knows best if and when they are hungry. Breastfeeding can be problematic sometimes because babies don't only ask for your breast when hungry but also when they are trying to go to sleep or are looking for comfort. Whenever your baby takes a leap, their familiar world is turned upside down, and your little one hangs on to what they already know. What better way to hang on than to literally attach to Mom's breast? You may find it deeply touching that your baby needs you so much, but there's the danger of your nipples hurting when your baby sucks too hard or too long.

DIET

Are painful nipples always a result of your baby seeking comfort by sucking more frequently?

It always depends on whether your nipples hurt just briefly or over a longer period of time. If your baby is visibly uncomfortable, such as during a leap, and demands your breast more often than usual, there's no reason to worry. You don't need to change anything about the way you're feeding. If it becomes too much, you need to distinguish between feeding and comforting. Try to comfort your baby another way. Sometimes it helps to warm your nipples shortly after feeding. You can do this with a blow dryer on the lowest setting. Also, let your nipples get some air as often as possible.

If sore nipples don't have anything to do with excessive sucking, there are usually three causes:

- Your baby doesn't suck well enough.

- Your baby is not in the optimal feeding position.

- You and your baby have thrush.

If your baby is not sucking well enough on your breast this may be a result of sucking on a pacifier or bottle that is not made for breastfed babies. Babies need a different sucking technique for these than for the breast, which leads to confusion. Therefore, in the beginning, you should refrain from using such products. Most often, your baby learns to suck properly on their own.

The right position is also very important because it makes it easier on your breasts. If you can't figure it out by experimenting, ask an expert at the clinic.

Thrush (Candida Albicans) is a fungal infection caused by yeasts and it affects approximately four percent of all babies. You can recognize the infection by small white spots in your baby's mouth. Your nipples may be sore and hurting too. Thrush is not dangerous but has to be treated. Visit your family practitioner if you suspect your baby has thrush.

Does my baby's mental development benefit if I eat lots of fish during pregnancy and while nursing?

Every baby takes leaps in development at the same time and acquires the same perceptive abilities. What babies use the new ability for is mainly determined by hereditary factors. However, Harvard Medical School in Boston has proven that during pregnancy and nursing a diet rich in fish promotes a baby's mental development. Babies are then better able to use the newly acquired perceptual ability. Please note that we're talking about fish that is low in mercury. The study also shows that high levels of mercury in the mother's blood have the opposite effect. Fish is healthy, so the positive impact on a baby's mental development makes sense.

DIET

Does bottle feeding versus breastfeeding have an impact on a baby's mental development?

Studies have shown that breastfeeding is preferable. Of course, you may not be able to nurse or decide against it. It doesn't have consequences for your baby's leaps. Babies take the same leaps at the same set times, and as parents, there is no difference in the way you handle the leaps with a breastfed baby than with a bottle-fed baby.

At what leap can I start with solid food?

You can start giving your baby solid food when they are between 4 and 6 months old. Of course, this is not a must. Some studies even disagree, saying that it's not recommend to give solid food this early. Various worldwide studies have shown that it's best to nurse a baby for six months before starting with solid food. If you don't breastfeed, give your baby formula until six months old. At this time, breast milk or formula is no longer enough and you have to introduce solid food. It doesn't have anything to do with a leap, but you probably shouldn't introduce a baby to their first spoon when the leap of "relationships" is about to happen. Babies take this leap around 26 weeks after the calculated delivery date, which is about six months. During a leap, your little one isn't quite at ease. It's difficult enough for a child that their whole world changes and they really don't need to be introduced to anything new. You're better off introducing your child to solid foods either *before* or *after* the leap. Also, don't start solid foods when your baby is sick.

Does a healthy diet have an impact on the leaps in development?

Eating well is always a good thing, especially when it comes to your child's mental development, no matter their age. Your child takes the leaps at set times whether they are eating healthy or not. The new things your child is going to do or not going to do with the perceptive ability acquired during a leap, however, are indirectly influenced by healthy food. An overweight child has to carry around more weight; therefore, that child probably doesn't run as fast or as well as children carrying less weight. Also, any attempts children take to master new skills require the brain to play along. As is generally known, the whole body works better when it's healthy and gets all the important nutrients.

Does drinking juice or water have an influence on mental development?

Once you start feeding solids at the age of six months, you'll probably let your baby drink from a sippy cup every now and then. Get your child used to a normal cup as soon as possible before the age of nine months. Not only is this much better for their teeth but it also promotes the development of chewing and speech. By providing optimal conditions for your child to learn how to talk, you help them master this skill to the best of their ability.

If my five-month-old baby suddenly puts everything in their mouth, is it a sign that I need to feed solids?

As soon as your baby has completed the leap of "events" (19 weeks after the calculated delivery date or four and a half months), you'll see that your baby puts things in their mouth more often, including your fingers, toys, and items lying around. At this point, everything is interesting to your baby and it's fun to put things in their mouth. This doesn't mean, however, that your baby is hungry but it's a logical consequence of this leap. Your baby investigates objects by feeling them with their lips and putting them in their mouth. You have to really pay attention to what your little one is investigating! If your baby puts things in their mouth that are dangerous, you need to warn them by saying "Ouch!" or "No!" Take the object from your baby and explain why you're doing it. Your baby won't understand exactly what you're talking about but they will learn that there are certain things they shouldn't put in their mouth.

At what age do babies show that they are hungry or full?

Starting at day one, your intuition tells you when your baby is hungry or has had enough to eat. The better you get to know your baby, the quicker you figure out which kind of crying means what. As soon as your baby has taken the leap of "events" (19 weeks after the calculated delivery date or four and a half months), your child will demonstrate hunger in a different way. Your baby will reach for your food or drink and make smacking sounds when they want to be breastfed or when they see the bottle. Many parents know their little one is full when their baby spits out the food or pushes the breast or bottle away. Your baby suddenly seems much more mature.

At what age do babies start having food preferences?

Under six months old babies pretty much like anything and don't have any preferences. Once your baby has taken the leap of "relationships" (26 weeks after the calculated delivery date or six months), you'll realize that your baby likes some foods better than others. Of course, this is great since it shows that your child is developing; food preferences represent a milestone as well. But all the fun is over when the preferences get to a point that the daily eating rituals turn into torture. A strong-willed child doesn't just let you know their preferences but simply refuses food they don't like. As parents, you'll start having doubts whether you're feeding your child well enough since you know that a variety is extremely important when it comes to eating healthy. However, make sure that this milestone doesn't become a constant issue. It doesn't do any good at all to make your child eat or to force healthy foods on the little one.

What can I do if my child refuses food?

Luckily, it's rare that foods, and sometimes even liquids, are refused to the point of malnourishment or dehydration. If you are worried that this is the case with your baby, contact your pediatrician immediately. Most often, it's a completely different and harmless form of food denial. For example, your child may deny the food because they prefer something else, they think it's funny that you're following them with the spoon, or they don't have an appetite because they are constantly being offered food by Mom or Dad. Therefore, never force your child to eat. If your child doesn't want to eat, set the food aside and offer it again a little later. Don't turn meals into a power game because your child will hold out longer than you will.

Also, keep in mind that we are talking about solid food here. Of course, solids contain nourishment, but initially, their main purpose is to get your baby used to different flavors and used to chewing and swallowing. As soon as solids become a primary source of nutrients, you may expect more of your little one when it comes to eating. At that point, you'll make the decisions when it comes to food, and you'll give your child a chance to signal you when they are full. If your child refuses the food but really didn't eat enough, don't give them a desert or a snack until they have eaten all the food on their plate. That way, you'll give your child a clear message that they will only get a desert once they have eaten the main course.

When do children start being able to eat by themselves?

Once your child has taken the leap of "sequences" (46 weeks after the calculated delivery date or 11 months), they understand that some things have to be done in a certain sequence in order to reach a certain goal. Given that your baby finds this skill interesting, you may see your child take a spoon full of food and move it towards their mouth during the period they are processing the leap. These are the first signs of independent eating. Of

course, you can't expect your baby to eat every meal on their own from now on. Give your baby the opportunity to try it over and over again even though it creates a big mess. If you notice that your little one gets tired or impatient, take the spoon and feed them the rest of the meal. Of course, you need to praise your child on how well they are eating on their own.

Is it important to let my child eat on their own?

It's always important to support your child's independency, and the efforts they make when learning something new. This pertains to eating and drinking as well. At some point, your baby will show you it's important to them to do these things without your help. With every leap in development that your child takes, "do-it-yourself" becomes increasingly important. Once your child has completed the leap of "sequences," "do-it-yourself" is a big deal. At that point, children want to eat by themselves when sitting at the dinner table. Some parents may lose patience when they see that more food ends up on the floor than in their child's mouth, or they agonize because their child really wants to eat unaided but the child gets completely frustrated because it doesn't work the way it's supposed to. Try to help your child in a positive way. Praise their efforts, or make a game of it. Take a spoon in your hand, and give another one to your baby. Your baby feeds you, and you feed your baby. That way your little one feels "big," and you're making sure that your baby still gets enough to eat.

When do I need to start paying special attention to healthy food?

Eating healthily is always important for mother and child, starting at pregnancy. You're not allowed to eat certain foods when pregnant because they're harmful to the baby. Once your child is allowed to snack, you really have to pay attention to healthy food since your child will try to get their hands on the yummy stuff and disregard "normal" food. So make it a habit from day one to pay attention to healthy food. Good nourishment pays off throughout life. By teaching your child early on, you'll help your child avoid health issues, including obesity and diabetes, later in life. Rule by example: eat health consciously!

Besides nutrients, what else do I have to pay attention to when it comes to eating and drinking?

Good nourishment supplies the body with all the important nutrients. However, eating and drinking are more than just taking in nutrients; they are also a social phenomenon. Make sure the whole family eats together at the table. Once your child is old enough, ask for help with anything pertaining to meals from grocery shopping to doing the dishes. By helping, your child not only gets the opportunity to take on some responsibility within the family but also subconsciously learns good eating habits. You can even teach your toddler to treat food sensibly in a playful way. Especially after the leap of "programs" (55 weeks after the calculated delivery date or 13 months), your child will be excited about the activities below and will be happy to help. Your child won't really understand some of the games until the leap of "principles" has been completed (64 weeks after the calculated delivery date or 15 months).

- ✓ Ask your child to help you take groceries from the shelves and put them in the shopping cart.

- ✓ Ask your child to help you put away the groceries at home.

- ✓ Ask your child to put their plate and silverware on the table. Children who have learned to walk early may be able to do this on their own. If your child is not walking or standing safely yet, they can help while sitting in the highchair. Give the child their plate, and ask them to put it on the table or the highchair tray.

- ✓ Ask your child to stir something for you.

- ✓ While you're cooking, give your child a few food items, a bowl with water, and a spoon. That way, your little one can "cook" something, too. Help them if you need to. Of course, you need to try it and say how delicious it is!

- ✓ Ask your child to help with the dishes. It's going to be lots of splashing but guaranteed fun for the both of you!

CHAPTER 6

Emotional Development

Secure Attachment Bonds, Fear of Strangers,
Separation Anxiety, Experiences and Feelings,
and Self-Confidence

Intelligence alone doesn't make you happy. The way someone stands in life, the joy they have in life, and the self-confidence they have are all aspects that determine a pleasant or less pleasant life. Your baby's emotional development, therefore, is no less important than their physical development. Give your baby a good start in life by being very conscious of their emotional development.

When does a child's emotional development start?

Although we know a lot about unborn babies, it's still difficult to analyze a baby's feelings in the womb. However, researchers are becoming more and more knowledgeable on the subject. Feelings are connected to the production of hormones, and this is already occurs in the womb. Therefore, feelings can be measured physically. Fright reactions are the visible results of feelings. Considering this, you can see and feel a baby has feelings in the mother's womb already. For instance, if there's a sudden loud noise close to you, your baby reacts with a severe turning movement or a kick. Some babies are even startled by an echo and hide their heads behind the pubic bone.

Do newborn babies already feel things like happiness, sadness, and pleasure?

Newborns experience the world as something like "soup." Everything the little ones perceive, sees, smells, tastes, or hears is one comprehensive experience, one big entity. Babies experience it in this way until the leap of "sensations" (five weeks after the calculated delivery date). Therefore, newborns don't only hear a loud noise but senses this unpleasant feeling with their whole body. All of a sudden, the baby is uncomfortable. Newborns also react with their whole body when it comes to pleasant things as well. Roughly speaking, babies experience everything as positive, negative, or neutral. The older babies get and the more leaps in development babies go through, the more the babies are able to distinguish feelings. A positive feeling can then be perceived as happiness, pleasure, love, etc. However, this doesn't mean that your newborn has fewer feelings and that you need to be less considerate of them. It's quite the opposite, especially since babies aren't able to separate the feelings into different emotions; babies' reactions are more severe now than they are later.

What does secure attachment bonds mean?

The expression already says it: to feel secure in relationships. To your baby, it refers to the relationship with you first and foremost. The little one needs this secure bond. Babies want to feel your unconditional love and know that you are always there for them because of who they are, not because of what they can and can't do. For newborns, this "feeling" is still natural. As long as there is skin contact, preferably belly-to-belly, and your baby hears your loving voice, everything's soon okay again. Once your baby becomes mobile and starts to go on excursions (from the secure base, which is you, of course), it's important that you are predictable, present, and available. Your child has to be able to trust that you'll still be there when they return from their excursions.

These excursions are very short at first and are often within your arm's reach. If you get up and walk away, your child becomes insecure and may hang on you. To be on the safe side, avoid walking away suddenly. During this phase, you often see babies whining and crawling after their parents or crying for their parents if they aren't able to crawl yet. The older your baby gets, the more complex the interactions between you and your child become. These interactions play a role in secure attachment bonds.

How do secure attachment bonds develop?

No one is born with secure attachment bonds; they develop over time. They can't be scheduled in your planner. You enable your baby to feel secure attachment bonds in everything you relay to your baby. The important thing is that you respect your baby's dignity and fulfill their needs in a loving manner. In the beginning, these needs are purely physical; later, they are more complex and are predominately mental needs.

How do I respect my child's dignity?

No mother or father would likely hurt their child's dignity on purpose. If parents make mistakes in this regard, it's not on an intentional act but usually occurs unknowingly. To avoid mistakes, you should always be aware of which step in mental development your baby is at. By thoroughly reading up on leaps in development, you'll get an increasingly better insight into your child's world and know what they understand and what they don't. If you take this into consideration, you'll find the key to your child's unique personality and will respect their dignity.

How do I fulfill my child's needs in a loving way?

Fulfilling your child's every need is not what makes parenting difficult, but discovering what the needs are in the first place is. If a child is whiny because they are not allowed to touch something, touching it seems to be the child's need. Your child probably thinks this is their greatest need right now. However, the real need is the need to learn rules. Fulfilling your child's needs doesn't mean that you have to go by what your child wants at all time.

What are every baby's primary emotional needs?

Starting on day one, a baby is busy with self-development and finding a place in society in a very primitive and subconscious way. However, the expressions "self-development" and "finding a place in society" reflect many primary emotional needs.

How do I bring my child's needs in accordance with my own?

In general, you'll realize that, with some dexterity, you'll satisfy both your and your child's needs. Secure attachment bonds don't mean that your child rules over all the other family members. A child needs to learn that Mom and Dad are sometimes busy with other things, and, therefore, the little one may have to wait now and then. A child understands this after the leap of "programs," which is at the age of about one year (also see Chapter 9, "Parenting," page 149).

Primary emotional needs for a child during "self-development:"

- ✓ Being exposed to games and situations pertaining to the things the child is fascinated with during a leap

- ✓ Parents who understand what their child is fascinated with and why something is interesting

- ✓ Parents who are there for their child when they're needed

- ✓ Parents who respect their child's dignity

- ✓ Parents who put the child's interests first

- ✓ The feeling the child is loved because of who they are, not because of what they can or can't do

- ✓ Realizing that a child is allowed to have feelings; a child is allowed to be sad or afraid when startled

- ✓ Parents who take a child's feelings seriously and are there for them

- ✓ Knowing where the child stands

- ✓ Feeling that the child is part of a bigger entity, a family

- ✓ Being allowed to be themselves

These are not all of your child's primary needs, by far. Secure attachment bonds aren't a list of ingredients with the end result being a perfect recipe. Secure attachment bonds form over the duration of one's life and continue to change and develop throughout life.

How do I handle my child's unpleasant experiences?

Every child experiences situations that aren't pleasant or that are even hurtful, both physically and emotionally. Of course, you try to avoid these situations as much as you can, but sometimes, you simply can't prevent them. For example, vaccinations are necessary for your child's health. Your child doesn't like being poked with the needle and doesn't understand why this has to happen. Some parents say their child still looks at them hours after the vaccination as if wanting to say, "You traitor." You then ask yourself whether the vaccination is at odds with secure attachment bonds. Vaccination is just one example, of course, and there are numerous other unpleasant situations that you don't have any control over. In this case, you have to tell yourself that these experiences may be unpleasant for the little one but are best for your child in the long run.

By accepting that you can't spare your child these experiences, you'll avoid panicking yourself and doubting your abilities as parents. Try to see the positive side. You can prove to your child that you are reliable and solid as a rock, especially during times of sadness and pain. Be considerate of your child's feelings and provide comfort. Calm your child with your voice and show empathy. Tell your child you understand that it hurts and that it's unpleasant. Let your little one cry about the pain, but be reassuring and say that the pain will go away.

Is there a connection between safe secure bonds and the completion of a leap in mental development?

The older your child gets, the longer the leap and bewilderment becomes. During this time, your child will be especially clingy, whiny, and moody. Your child cries a lot and always wants to be near you. The leap turns the familiar world upside down, so your child hangs on to you as the familiar person. Of course, this is more pronounced in some babies than in others, but for the parents, it remains a difficult and sometimes frustrating time. It's best to provide secure attachment bonds by first understanding that the confusion is not your baby's fault. Your baby is under an enormous amount of stress when taking a leap; so your child literally screams for safety and comfort from you during this difficult phase.

What can I do if my child gets on my nerves too much or if I'm so tired that it's difficult for me to show unconditional love?

The difficult phase during the leaps also takes its toll on the parents, and some parents realize they're reaching the limit of what they can endure. All of a sudden, you slap your child, which is against all your beliefs. If it has come to that, you have really gone too far, and you have taken it out on your child. You've hurt your child's dignity, which doesn't promote positive secure attachment bonds. Your child depends on you, and you have to be reasonable.

There's no shame in recognizing you have limits. It's actually the opposite; it's good and will contribute to secure attachment bonds. Take precautions when it's really getting to be too much for you. Ask someone to watch your baby for a few hours while you go for a walk or take a nap. Make sure that your batteries get fully recharged, so you can commit to giving your child loving care again.

What do a fear of strangers and separation anxiety mean?

Once a baby has taken the leap of "relationships," (around six months of age), many parents notice that all of a sudden, their child isn't as comfortable in the presence of strangers anymore. The child seems to be afraid of them and hangs on to the person they're most comfortable with. The term "strangers" is used in the widest sense of the word. One baby is skittish with the neighbor who knows the baby while another is only skittish with people they have never met before. This fear of strangers may last between six months and one year, and for some children, until the age of two years. Children's fear of other people is often connected with the fear of being separated from the person the child relates most closely with, and for your child that is you, of course. Suddenly, your baby is afraid when you leave the room or even move to another area of the room. It's because your child now understands they have lost control of keeping you in close proximity to them. This fear is called separation anxiety.

What can I do about my child's separation anxiety?

Help your baby understand that even though you're out of sight sometimes, you're still there for them. For instance, keep talking when you leave the room, so your baby hears your voice and knows that you're still there even if they can't see you anymore. You can also use games to teach your baby that something is still there even if it's not visible. For example, put a towel over a toy, and ask your baby, "Where's the toy?" Then pull the towel away, and in a happy voice, say, "There's the toy!" Your baby will like this little game, especially after completing the leap of "relationships." You can play endless varieties of these simple types of hiding games.

How can I help my baby get through the skittish phase?

First of all, you have to understand that fear of strangers is perfectly normal, and it's important to not dismiss your child's fears as nonsense. However, you shouldn't feel you need to spare your baby's feelings during this phase by avoiding strangers as much as possible. Keep inviting people you would normally invite, and visit them if you feel like it. Ask your visitors or hosts to leave your baby alone at first. Keep your baby on your lap for a little while, and let your baby decide themselves at what point they want to approach others or gradually leave the safe spot of Dad or Mom's lap to sit somewhere else or to crawl around. Always let your baby take the lead. Allow your little one to decide when others can approach them. That way, you're giving your child a chance to overcome the fear on their own, which is a good investment for further development. In the short run, you reduce

the time of skittishness and make it easier to deal with, and in the long run, you help your child become self-confident.

Can I take my child to a daycare center if they are afraid of strangers?

If your child is very skittish right now, it's not the best time to promote their independency. It's better to get your child used to a babysitter or daycare center either before or after this phase.

Also, keep in mind that babies who are already going to a daycare center and are used to it may suddenly not want to go there anymore or may become afraid of the caretaker. Talk to your babysitter or caretaker about your child's current skittishness. Ask the person to cuddle your child or leave them alone when you're leaving. Whether the caretaker cuddles your baby or leaves them alone depends on the child's preferences, and you're only able to find out by trying different scenarios. You may want to call the babysitter or caretaker half an hour after you leave and ask how your child is doing. It will make you feel better in any case.

What should I do if my child is afraid of strangers and only wants to be with me, but I really have to leave for a moment?

At some point, your child will experience that you have to leave for a little while without them. Every child will eventually have a problem with this and will make it quite clear to you that they do not agree with the situation. Here are some tips to make the parting easier for your child:

✓ Tell your child in clear, understandable words that you have to leave for a little while but that you'll be right back. You could also say where you're going. Be brief and don't turn it into a long story; otherwise, you'll create uncertainty in your child.

✓ Give your child a big kiss, say goodbye, and leave. If you let your child upset you through their crying or other kind of protest, your child will notice, which makes saying goodbye even more difficult.

✓ Never sneak off. By doing that, you're are teaching your child that you could suddenly disappear if they don't always keep an eye on you, therefore worsening separation anxiety.

Can you teach toddlers self-confidence?

Self-confidence is something toddlers are able to experience to some extent around the age of one to two years, but it isn't experienced consciously until children are older. Self-confidence is really a feeling. However, you can set the foundation for this feeling from the cradle by supporting your baby during their development. Expose your baby to various situations that require your baby's effort. Let your baby try out things that are within their capabilities, yet that are challenging at the same time and that are difficult but never too difficult. That way, your baby learns early on that they can do things when they make the effort. You can help by creating surroundings that provide your child with a chance to be successful through their efforts. For instance, you may put a toy where your baby can easily reach it and practice grabbing. You may keep the distance between you and another person so short that your baby is able to walk from the one person to the other in just two steps. This gives your baby the feeling of actually having walked a short distance all on their own, making your little one and you, of course, tremendously proud! You need to show how proud you are by extensively praising and encouraging your child in a happy voice, but you must also praise your baby even if something doesn't work out. In this case, you're simply proud of your little sweetie's efforts. Children and their self-confidence grow with encouragement, success, and praise!

Why is self-confidence so important? And why do you have to start working on it from early childhood?

Self-confidence is one of the most important requirements for creating a successful and secure life. Self-confidence goes hand-in-hand with self-knowledge and knowledge of one's own limits. A girl with a healthy self-confidence won't easily get into a perilous situation. A boy with a healthy self-confidence won't easily be convinced to participate in stupid and dangerous activities. People who were "fed" self-confidence early on know, and are able to set their limits later in life.

How do I act towards my child when there's stress at home?

Babies have very fine antennae that picks up the atmosphere at home and within the family, and sometimes, there may be stress, including trouble at work, illness of a family member, or a break-in. There are lots of worries and problems we don't have any influence on. These could cause a stressful day for the parents, but the period of stress might last longer, as is the case with grief, for instance. You are not your usual self and don't feel well, and your baby senses it. You can't avoid these kinds of situations, but you can make them as bearable as possible for everyone. First of all, accept the situation for what it is. It doesn't do any good to hide your feelings. Deliberately plan more calmness in your daily routine, especially within the areas you have influence on.

CHAPTER 7

Stress

Problems and Disagreements
in Parenting, Doubts, Overextension,
and Stress Reduction

Having a baby is one of the most beautiful experiences in life and leads to the biggest changes in life. Nothing is the way it was before. Planning your daily routine, your values in life, and your energy levels all change; everything changes. In short, you see the world through different eyes, which sometimes causes great tension for you and your family. The tension shows itself in moments of despair, during times of emotional distress, and during arguments or alienation between you and your partner, your other children, your parents, or your in-laws. These are unpleasant moments of parenthood, but they are part of it and perfectly normal.

Is it normal that as a parent I'm sometimes downright desperate?

Sometimes, your baby may demand a lot of you during the difficult phase of a leap in development. Babies don't do this on purpose but it's instinctive. Your child's whole world is turned upside down, and there's confusion. Therefore, your little one resorts to the one pillar, Mom and/or Dad. Your child literally hangs on to you. Although you know you have to be there for the child, you might react pretty annoyed, or you might be overcome by a feeling of helplessness. It's still a taboo for many parents to admit this, and they have other parents' statements on their minds saying *they* never have any problems with it. The fact is, of course, that most mothers and fathers know these feelings quite well. Whenever your baby takes a leap, your patience is put to a severe test. You're only human, so accept that you can get pretty desperate every now and then. Discuss your feelings with your partner. Don't take your frustration out on your baby! Admitting feelings of despair and accepting and talking about them proves that you're a good parent. You'll realize that this eases the stress and makes it easier on your baby and your whole family.

How can I avoid being stressed when my child is about to go through a leap?

First and foremost, you have to accept the fact that leaps are part of a baby's development and that these phases are not pleasant for your baby; therefore, they have an effect on you, your partner, and your other children. You can prepare for a leap if you know what's going on in your baby's little head and what your little one is up against. Preparing yourself for the leaps shortens the difficult period and reduces the stress for you, your baby, and your whole family.

What can I do if it seems like everything is getting too much for me?

Parenthood demands a lot of you, mentally and physically. Whenever your baby is going through a leap, you may get the feeling every now and then that you've reached your limit, and sometimes, it's the last straw that breaks the camel's back. Some parents have tears of despair and exhaustion in their eyes. You get to a point where you realize that everything is becoming too much. We are not talking about those stressful moments when you're briefly fed up and back to laughing in five minutes. It's very important you are able to distinguish between a touch of resignation and true emotional distress. A moment of despair is often solved by a good cry in the arms of your comforting partner. A longer and more severe low is not overcome as easily or quickly, of course. If possible, try to not let it get to that point. Don't only have your baby's wellbeing in mind but your own as well. Make sure you tell yourself that your health is also important for your child's wellbeing. After all, a happy Mom and Dad are able to pass on more happiness to their child than unhappy parents. Recognize your limits, and don't be afraid to tell your partner or your doctor when you have reached your limit.

How do you avoid true mental distress?

Some people are more sensitive to stress than others, and some get to the point of mental distress a little easier than others. The reason for the difference doesn't really matter much here. It's about how you prevent getting into mental distress or getting depressed for your own interest, your child's interest, and your family's interest. It's important to recognize the symptoms early on. If you realize that a mental low is about to happen, you need to raise the alarm immediately. Come up with a plan to get out of the stress spiral. Ask your partner for more help with the baby, and make note of these days on your calendar. Do something fun during these times, go for a walk, go swimming, or indulge in shopping. Don't feel guilty in the least about taking these timeouts. By being considerate to yourself, you avoid getting into severe mental distress and not being able to fulfill your baby's needs. Don't shy away from discussing depression with your family practitioner or someone at a consultation center.

Is it bad if my baby sees me crying?

Your baby senses how you're feeling if you're sad and if you're crying. In the beginning, babies literally even taste your feelings through the breast milk, so it's not about the tears that are flowing but the feeling that comes with them. Your baby would rather see you happy and cheerful because then they're happy and cheerful, too. This doesn't mean that you aren't allowed to cry in your baby's presence, but every now and then, you just have to pull yourself together. Whenever you're sad, it's a good idea to let your baby know that it's not because of them. Cuddle your little one, smile, and try to replace your tears with feelings of happiness as quickly as you can.

How do you get to know yourself and your partner as a new couple after a baby is born?

Up until the birth of your child, you knew each other solely as a man and a woman who have been together for some time. This changes completely the moment you have a baby. You now have something unique together and share a responsibility. Never before have you experienced responsibility to this extent. You are deeply touched by your baby, and you realize that your partner feels the same. The type of men who usually throw their weight around, walk around for days with tears of joy in their eyes, and the most self-confident women may suddenly have doubts with every diaper they change. It seems like you were born again when your baby was born. A woman is reborn as mother and a man as a father. Often, you realize a few months after the birth of your child that you've gotten pretty used to the new role.

STRESS

How do you handle disagreements regarding a baby's care during the first few months?

Since there are so many new things ahead that neither of you have any experience with, it's completely normal that it takes you a while to find the right approach to handling your offspring. During the first few months after birth, the focus is often on how to establish your new life effectively. Many disagreements are about sleeping, crying, feeding, and experimenting with the leaps in mental development. You have to look for strategies that are acceptable to you as well as your partner. Love and comfort are amongst the elementary things to give to your baby, and you have to rule by example. Two stressed out parents who are constantly fighting have never contributed to a relaxed atmosphere at home. Communication, as banal as it may sound, is the only thing that really helps you two get on the same page. While your baby is sleeping, agree to talk about everything and take your time when doing so. Be understanding of your partner's opinions because both of you want the best for your baby.

Is it normal that my partner and I argue more often when our baby is going through a leap?

When your baby cries a lot, or doesn't sleep or feel well, it takes a toll on the whole family. A leap is tough on your baby; therefore, your baby is difficult to handle. As a parent, you're bewildered, thinking something could be wrong. Your sleep is interrupted because your baby wakes up a lot. After a few days filled with worries and little sleep, your stress level has reached its limit. So, the leap in mental development doesn't only result in your baby going through a difficult phase, but it's also a tough time for you. The spiral keeps going. When Mom or Dad is stressed, it naturally has an impact on the whole family. Of course, this doesn't improve the atmosphere at home, which a baby who's already very sensitive picks up on. Your baby then becomes even more "difficult." You see, a leap has far-reaching consequences!

What do I do if my partner and I want to handle a difficult phase for our baby in different ways?

There's no doubt that it's always better when Dad and Mom agree, especially during difficult times. When your baby is going through a leap and is flustered all day long, doesn't eat well, cries a lot, and doesn't sleep much, it leads to testiness in both of you before long. There are many lasting decisions you have to agree on, but a leap is something that comes and goes, so keep this in mind when discussing how to proceed. You can plan ahead and determine how you want to handle the situation and distribute the responsibilities together. The questions below may be helpful in drawing up an appropriate plan. There's no right or wrong answer; the answer you agree on is the right one.

How do you find time for one another with all the stress of a baby?

You clearly have less time to spend alone together than you had before your baby was born, and that's putting it mildly. It is now out of the question to go to the movies on a whim. If you want to be alone together, you have to do so while your baby's asleep or hire a babysitter. In the beginning, this takes some getting used to. Most often, women are not the ones that have a problem with it, but it's the men who miss the former affection from their partner. Of course, not every man makes a big deal out of it, and it doesn't mean there aren't women who miss the familiar closeness with their partner. In any case, you need to talk about it because your relationship is also important for your baby. If one of you wants more togetherness, you should agree to that. Agree on arrangements that suit you both. Your baby will sense your positive attitude towards one another.

When can I start letting a babysitter watch my child?

From a practical point of view, there's nothing wrong with entrusting your baby to a babysitter immediately after birth. Whether it's desirable is another story. In the beginning, it's very important for you and your baby to spend a lot of time together. You have to get used to one another, which doesn't happen overnight. It really is best for your baby to feel your presence as often as possible. That way, you form a tight bond, and you give your baby the basic feeling of security and comfort. "As often as possible" is difficult to define, though. What is "as often as possible?" On the one hand, your baby is the highest priority. On the other hand, there are things that you can't do when your baby is with you or you have obligations you have to meet. In this case, you don't have a choice but to entrust your baby to a babysitter.

Sleep

✓ Do you always put your baby to bed at the same time whether your baby is tired or not?

✓ If your baby doesn't want to sleep, after how many minutes should you go and get them?

✓ Should you stay in your baby's room until they are asleep?

✓ Do you think you spoil your baby if you respond to their crying?

✓ Who puts your baby to bed?

✓ Who gets up at night when your baby cries?

✓ How about whoever gets up at night the most during the week gets to stay in bed on weekends?

✓ Should breast milk be expressed, so Mom doesn't always have to get up and can sleep through the night every now and then?

✓ Is there someone living close by who could come by for an hour every once in a while, so you can take a powernap during the day?

Crying

✓ Do you let your baby cry every now and then?

✓ Do you both agree on the extent of comfort?

✓ Do you both agree on the methods of comforting your baby?

✓ When it comes to comforting, what are the differences between you and your partner, and could you learn something from each other?

✓ Do you both think that you really have to be there for your baby when they are going through a difficult phase even though it's sometimes at the expense of the attention you pay to yourself or your partner?

✓ Do you both agree that your baby cries more due to a leap, or does one of you doubt the reason for crying? (When in doubt, always contact a doctor or consultation center.)

Diet

✓ Do you both agree on the food your baby gets (breast or bottle)?

✓ If you breastfeed, have you discussed what this means for a mother?

✓ If you breastfeed, does your partner know this may be a physically difficult task?

✓ If you breastfeed, is there something your partner can do to help with feeding?

✓ Are you unsure if your baby takes in enough food? (When in doubt, always ask a doctor.)

✓ Do you agree on the amount of solid food you give your baby?

✓ Do you agree on how to handle your baby's refusal to eat during a leap?

Stress relief

✓ Do you both agree the stress is due to a leap? (When in doubt, contact a doctor or consultation center.)

✓ When it comes to parenting, are the responsibilities evenly distributed?

✓ Do you agree that raising children uses up a lot of energy even when they're still very young?

✓ Is it an option that your partner spends more time with the baby when they are getting too much for you?

Does every leap have a big impact on the whole family?

Not every leap has the same effect on every baby. The first leaps happen quickly and have less of an impact on the family than the following leaps. The older your baby gets, the longer the leaps last. Therefore, the periods of time during which your child doesn't sleep will last longer, too. Nevertheless, even the first leaps might disrupt domestic harmony, especially if this is your first baby and you don't have any previous experience as a parent, are insecure, doubt yourself, or worry about your baby's health. With doubts comes stress, which affects the other family members.

Can I prepare my other children for our baby's leap?

It makes sense that your baby's leap is implicitly difficult for any other children in the family as well. Depending on the siblings' ages, you might be able explain to them what's going on with your baby. Starting at the age of four years, children understand this. It's best is to come up with a little story about what's changing in baby's head. Of course, you don't need to explain every little detail because this would be too difficult for a child to understand. However, the child understands that the baby has to learn a lot right now, and that's why the baby's whole world is changing at the moment. Your children can even help out. For instance, ask the older children to help you distract or comfort the baby by drawing or crafting something for the little one.

How can I make sure that the amount of attention I am giving to my baby is not at my other children's expense?

Spreading time and devotion evenly is an art of its own. More than likely, you'll hear from your older children that you're doing it wrong, no matter how hard you try. The oldest might complain that you're constantly busy with the baby while the younger ones can become whiny again in order to get your attention. Try to include your baby when playing the games you always played with your older children before baby was born. Your baby will love being involved when you're doing crafts with your other children. Carry your little one in a sling or put the bouncer next to you. While you're spending time crafting with your other children, talk to your baby often and show them the crafts you're making. That way, your older children won't have a reason to protest since you're spending time with them, too. Your baby will enjoy being part of and watching a happy group. You can even incorporate leaps in these activities. For example, when showing your baby the craft you're working on, carefully use it to fan the little one; that way, you incorporate the leap of "smooth transitions" (at about 12 weeks of age). Or during the leap of "events" (at about 19 weeks of age), you could take a piece of paper and make a rustling sound while allowing your baby to feel how it crackles. If your baby is currently trying to sit, place your little one next to you with the support of your nursing pillow. That way, you'll have your hands free to craft while your baby is having fun learning to sit. You see, with a little creativity, you'll be able to please everyone!

How do I explain to my other children that the baby is allowed to do certain things that they aren't allowed to do?

Starting at the age of 18 months, children realize that there are differences and that their little brother or sister is sometimes allowed to do things that they are not allowed to do. Although a children's brain is able to understand this, it doesn't necessarily mean that they agree to the fact. Explain to your other children that the baby is not as developed as they are, so you expect more from them than from a little baby. Repeat this message clearly during every discussion.

How do I handle it when my in-laws' opinions regarding parenting are different from mine?

When your parents or in-laws were raising their children, they did it their way. Now that you have children, you do it your way. When it comes to parenting, the important thing is that everyone does what works for them. Feel free to take good advice from parents who are a little more experienced, but don't let it get to you. In the past, only one generation earlier, crying was shrugged off as belly cramps, babies were fed at set times instead of on demand, and much less was known about babies' mental development. In recent years, lots of research has been done regarding how babies develop. Nowadays, we know significantly more. However, for some reason, many grandparents feel the need to voice their unsolicited opinions. It's really absurd considering that *their* parents probably got on their nerves doing the same thing. Take the advice calmly. Avoid these discussions when possible, but when they do occur, deal with the advice however you please. Realize that the advisors probably want the same thing for your baby as you do: only the best.

STRESS

My parents watch my baby but do things I absolutely don't want them to do. How should I make it clear to them?

Usually, it's easy to express your concerns to a babysitter or a caretaker when there's something you don't agree with. After all, you are the parents and are entitled to make the decisions. It's a little bit more delicate when it's your parents who are doing something that you don't agree with while watching the baby. The older generation has their own idea when it comes to parenting, and if you criticize them, you are indicating that something was wrong with the way you were raised. However, it is important to stick to your personal principles regarding raising your baby. Explain to your parents that society has changed; and therefore parenting has changed, too. That way, they won't feel attacked. You won't be able to blame everything on social changes, though; this is when you need to remain steadfast in your opinion. If there are serious differences, you may want to ask yourself whether or not you'd be better off looking for another babysitter.

CHAPTER 8

Intelligence

Interests, Personality, Thinking,
Stimulating, and Support

As parents, you want the best for your baby. You're secretly hoping for an intelligent child with a successful future in store. What is intelligence, though? Does intelligence really have anything to do with success, and how do you assess a baby's preferences and interests? Even more importantly, is it really necessary for parents to focus on the baby's preferences and interests?

What is intelligence?

Intelligence is a big word that's actually often used incorrectly. At mentioning the word, intelligence quotients and the corresponding good grades in school spring to mind. True intelligence, of course, goes way beyond success in school. Today, we know with increasing certainty that there is not only one form of intelligence but multiple forms. The founder of this theory is Howard Gardner. According to him, there are eight different forms of intelligence:

1. Musical intelligence

2. Bodily-kinesthetic intelligence (the ability to utilize the body or parts of the body when playing, performing in various kinds of sports, or expressing emotions as in ballet or other forms of dance)

3. Logical-mathematical intelligence (talented at math)

4. Linguistic intelligence

5. Spatial intelligence (the ability to think in three dimensions or spatial overview)

6. Interpersonal or social intelligence (the ability to recognize intentions and desires of others even when not said out loud)

7. Intrapersonal intelligence (the ability to understand one's own feelings and use them to direct actions)

8. Naturalist intelligence (the ability to understand animals and plants in a special way).

Do babies have all the forms of intelligence?

Your baby has every form of intelligence within themselves. The question is which forms are most developed. Starting at birth, your baby has an inclination for one or several forms of intelligence. This will become more and more obvious to you the older your baby gets. However, it's still a little early to use the word intelligence. In babies and young children, it's better to speak of interests and skills. The terms "interests" and "skills" are more useful to you as parents. With your ability to recognize your baby's interests and focus on stimulating those interests, your baby will easily develop inherent talents. The intention is not to turn your baby into a smart child but into a happy one. Your baby wants to be supported in the things they're fascinated with and interested in, just like everyone else.

Why is it so important that I pay attention to my child's interests?

During the first few years, you and your child get to know each other. If you observe carefully, your baby's unique personality will reveal itself to you with increasing clarity, and this is, without a doubt, the most beautiful "expedition" you'll ever go on in your life. Part of the personality you'll get to know on this expedition is what things your baby is interested in. These things play a role in determining the how a baby will develop, including how a baby handles leaps, masters skills, and accepts new challenges. You see, your baby's interests are certainly one of the most important aspects you need to focus on during development since they determine how the various forms of intelligence develop. Always keep in mind that your baby is the one who has to find their own interests, and they may not necessarily coincide with yours. Always let your child show you what they are interested in, and don't force anything on your child that you like. It sounds quite self-explanatory, but it's actually one of the most difficult things in parenting.

How can I determine my child's interests and skills?

After every leap, your child achieves another new perceptual ability with the result of being able to develop many new skills. A child subconsciously chooses what to master first. What a child chooses reveals their interests and skills, and, therefore, it reveals something about their personality. After a few leaps, you'll notice that your baby is usually most interested in the same kind of skills. For one child, it may be all motor (bodily-kinesthetic) skills, and for another, it could be interpersonal interests and so on. It is too early, though, to draw conclusions for later life, especially since your baby is still in the midst of developing. However, keep the apparent interests in mind and respond to them by playing games with your child according to their interests.

How do I know what my child is already able to do and understand and what is still too difficult?

People are most content when there's balance in life and when there's no boredom. At the same time, they don't like having to do things that are too difficult and demanding. Your child wants to be approached on their level. You do your child the biggest favor by being aware of their level of development and by responding accordingly. Take your time to get to know your child and observe carefully. The older your child gets, the more you'll notice that your little one sometimes gets bored with something and is longing for a new challenge. On the flip side, you may notice that your child is frustrated because of things they don't understand or are unable to do. The more you devote yourself to your child, the better you'll figure out what their interests and abilities are. You'll also discover what's considered a welcomed challenge, what tasks are too difficult, what's too easy and boring, and what your child doesn't want to do anymore.

Tip

Never demand too much of your child, no matter their age. Appreciate your child the way they are. When you ask something of your child, make sure it's something they can do, and stimulate them in a way that meets your child's interests.

Is there a way to find out whether my child will have a high IQ later in life?

There is no checklist that can help you determine early on what intelligence quotient your child will have at the age of six or older, which is good. However, there's research being done on how this form of intelligence can be predicted at an early age. In the course of the research, circumstances have been discovered suggesting that it may be possible to predict whether a baby will be highly intelligent or skilled later in life based on a number of indicators.

Your baby:

- Is demanding and not easily satisfied
- Cries a lot (also see Chapter 4, "Crying," page 75)
- Is easily bored
- Is constantly searching for a new challenge
- Is able to be occupied with something in deep concentration for a long time
- Observes a lot
- "Practices" in their head
- Predominantly successful on the first attempt when trying something new
- Demands more attention than other babies do
- Has highly developed fine motor skills on their level (also see Chapter 2, "Physical Development," page 33)

Always keep in mind that these are solely indicators. Not every demanding baby possesses a high intelligence and vice versa. Parents are better off trusting their intuition and simply keeping these indicators in mind.

Can little babies be demanding?

Everyone knows that newborn babies do not sleep around the clock to give parents a chance to do what they want to do, unlike what stories suggest. The fact is that only very few newborn babies sleep eight hours at a time and lie peacefully in their little beds during the time they're awake. Most parents have the feeling that their baby shows their needs soon after birth. The baby wants to be held, to be nursed (without being hungry), to look at their surroundings, and is bored when in the same spot for too long. You'll notice it even more after the first leap, which occurs approximately five weeks after the calculated delivery date. With every leap, your baby wants to learn more about life, and this is how it's supposed to be. Therefore, it's perfectly normal that you notice your baby is demanding more and more. The parents then feel like they're on their last leg and are desperately searching all day long for ways to satisfy their baby. They discover, for instance, that their baby is very interested in a certain picture in the room. For five minutes, the baby looks at the picture with big eyes, finally seems to be happy, and falls asleep. Upon waking and becoming restless, the picture is suddenly not interesting any more. The parents, once again, have to search for something else that might interest their baby. It then seems as if the baby looked

at the picture, processed it in the brain, and "put it aside." The baby needs new stimulation and is restless until being offered something new that's interesting. Babies like this are called demanding. To a lot of people, the word "demanding" has a negative ring, but it really should be an inspiring, nice challenge for parents to raise a child who wants to get everything out of life that it has to offer. This is actually great, isn't it?

How do you prevent boredom in babies?

All babies want to learn; they want to discover the world, and they are fascinated with anything new to them. If your baby gets bored, it just means that your little one is telling you that "I understand this already, and now, I'd like to see or experience something different." With some babies it is clearly obvious that they are bored because they cry and become restless. That's your signal that your baby is looking for a new challenge. Other babies make it less obvious that they're bored and may become somewhat withdrawn. It's especially important for parents of these babies to interpret the behavior correctly. That the baby is not showing a loud and clear interest in new things doesn't mean that the little one doesn't have a desire for them; the desire is definitely there! Explore together what your child is fascinated with, wants to discover, feels like doing, and wants to be challenged with.

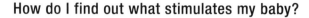

How do I find out what stimulates my baby?

First of all, you need to get to know your baby well. Over time, you will find out what fascinates your baby, what they find boring, and what's still too difficult and challenging. You'll never know with 100 percent certainty, no matter how hard you try. Your baby develops quickly, and factors stimulating your baby to master certain skills change just as quickly. However, this is what makes the whole thing so enjoyable for your baby and you. Basically, the whole family is busy discovering all the new things with your baby. For instance, your baby finds out that a rubber ball bounces and moves up and down. Something you took for granted is a fun game to your baby, and baby's excitement over the bouncing ball transfers to you. Because of your baby, you get to know the world in a new way.

By delving into the leap your baby is currently going through, you'll get clues regarding the challenges your baby will pursue. You are informed about what's going on in their little head and what new skills come with the leap. So one week before your baby takes a leap, read the pertaining chapter in this book and start thinking about what your baby is about to learn. Contemplate whether the conditions at home are right to implement the leap or if you need to do or change something beforehand. By preparing for the leap and adjusting to what your baby is fascinated with during this phase and what stimulates their interest, it will be easier for your baby to accomplish the leap.

How do I find the right amount of challenge for my baby?

A child wants to be challenged on their level in an appealing way. If the bar is set to high or low, a baby gets frustrated. If you force your child to play in a way that doesn't match your child's personality, don't be surprised when your child doesn't participate with excitement. Your baby is the one who decides whether a new challenge is welcome or not. If you push too hard and try to stimulate too much, which demands too much from your child, the consequences are negative rather than positive. This actually applies to everything regarding development. Don't offer anything; instead, let your child choose. Don't force anything on your child that's not interesting or that's too difficult.

Why does my baby suddenly seem startled or frightened by something that they actually find fascinating?

Your baby is interested in anything new. Your baby suddenly understands this new thing due to the leap that gave them the ability to do so. The new thing is challenging, and at the same time, a new world opens up to your baby. Your child's interest is aroused because the brain longs to discover new things. It still is perfectly normal that your baby seems reluctant or afraid of the new thing now and then. Your baby is more or less aware that they don't really know the game that's being played or they don't understand the feeling they suddenly have. Your baby's senses are being assaulted by so many new impressions and they become afraid or startled by all the new things. Generally, a child will not act fearfully but will close their eyes or look away. The little one needs a brief, quiet moment to process what's going on. If you notice this reaction in your baby, let them have that moment. Also, let your baby indicate when they have had enough rest. Sometimes, it's only a few seconds; other times, it takes longer. Your baby knows exactly how much time is needed to process the new impressions, so let your baby lead you.

Is it unusual that a baby is completely fascinated with something and can't get any rest because of it?

Most babies clearly show when rest is needed. The new game is fun to them, but when they are getting tired, they give in to fatigue. However, after having accomplished a leap, some babies are so interested in their new skills that they want to try out everything at all costs, and keep going until they achieved their goal and mastered the new skills. These babies demand a lot from their parents but also demand a lot from themselves. That's why they sometimes need to be protected from themselves. Try to find situations that allow your baby to engage in the new skills that come with a leap but also to calm down.

INTELLIGENCE

Is it normal that my baby is occupied for hours at a time with something irrelevant?

What seems irrelevant to us may be tremendously interesting to a baby. You're not the first parent to discover that your baby finds that the most fascinating thing about that fancy toy with all the different functions is actually the label that's stuck to it. Your baby has an eye for detail. Your little one may be completely fascinated by the most irrelevant things. Since these may be trivial to us, some parents think that their baby is dull. Some even draw the conclusion that their baby is autistic because the little one steadily strokes a step with their little fingers or keeps twisting a reel of thread for hours at a time. Parents are inclined to assume the worst, but that assumption is usually unfounded. Being occupied with something trivial for hours at a time is certainly no reason to doubt your child's intelligence or health. It's quite the opposite; your baby's brain is working hard. Your baby is discovering the world's basic laws. For example, by stroking the step, the baby familiarizes themselves with the material and their surroundings and also experiences the fundamental forces at that moment by moving their finger across a certain spot. By twisting a reel of thread, which means making very subtle movements with the hand, a baby sees the object in various ways. We know that something looks different from a different angle even though it's still the same thing. Your baby is discovering this while twisting the reel. This is actually clever!

Is the brain being stimulated when you talk a lot to a baby?

Your baby enjoys your dialogue even at a very young age. Your little one listens to your voice and looks at your face. This is calming and comforting to a baby. With these intense "conversations," a baby practices seeing, hearing, listening, smelling, and moving. Talk to your baby as often as possible, and start this right after birth because soon after birth the cerebrum starts rapidly creating neuronal branches. The more connections, the better the information is transmitted. By talking a lot to your child, you stimulate interaction, and this interaction ensures the connections will be preserved. As crazy as it may sound, the newly formed connections can die off if not used.

Is a baby's brain stimulated by exposing a baby to many new experiences?

As a matter of fact, your baby longs for new experiences. Nobody is as curious and eager to learn as a baby. Animal studies have shown that neuronal connections form when stimulated by experiences early on. We are using the term "experiences" in the widest sense of the word. It's about a baby hearing, seeing, and experiencing new things. In the past, it was assumed that very

young babies are not able to do anything; therefore, they were left for hours at a time in their little beds without any attention. The common thought was that babies weren't able to learn yet. Nowadays, we know better. Therefore, talk to your baby, let your little one embrace their surroundings, react to your baby's signals, and allow your baby be a part of your family and everyday activities as much as possible. That way, you stimulate the formation of neuronal connections in the brain. Think of it this way: you'll get back double and triple the energy you invest in the form of an active and happy child who's eager to learn. By putting your baby aside all the time without interaction, you raise a child who does not want to do anything and who hardly interacts.

Does the way I treat my baby have any effect on their IQ later in life?

In fact, the intelligence quotient is partially influenced by the way you treat your baby. For the most part, it is determined at the time of conception, and there is clear evidence that IQ is hereditary. However, you are able to influence it positively as well as negatively, and it starts with pregnancy. As is already known, smoking is not only harmful to you and your baby's health but it also has an immediate negative effect on your baby's IQ. The same applies for the time after birth because babies takes in harmful substances when drinking breast milk and by breathing in the

smoke. Besides the physical effects, the amount of stimulation you've provided early on plays a role in IQ as well. This was proven in a study done on children in a daycare center where caregivers did hardly anything or even nothing at all with the babies. They didn't pay much attention to the babies, who were mainly lying in their little beds staring at a boring white ceiling. Years later, when the children's IQ was measured, it was indeed lower than in another group of babies that were sufficiently stimulated.

Does going to a daycare center have an influence on my baby's IQ?

Everything around your baby and everyone taking care of your baby influences your baby's development, including IQ and how much stimulation is being provided to develop your baby's interests. A bad daycare center has a certain impact on your baby's development. However, the same applies to a babysitter or even you! Getting everything they need from every direction is very important for your baby, including experiences with their surroundings and the time a baby needs to discover them. It's more difficult when you entrust your baby to a babysitter or a daycare center. Sometimes, your child is treated differently than you would like. Discuss your concerns with the management of the daycare center or with the babysitter, and try to work out a plan. If you realize that you can't come to an agreement, you are better off looking for another babysitter or daycare center even if this creates logistic problems. Your baby is more important.

At what point do babies start thinking consciously?

"Consciously" is a very difficult term. Even in adults, "consciously" can't really be described. If thinking of it in terms of "purposefully," it's a little easier to understand. With every leap in development, babies sets more complex goals. Their purposefulness is becoming increasingly similar to ours. In the past, babies were considered to be born barren, which means a body consisting of bones and muscles with skin around them that's equipped with a few reflexes. Fortunately nowadays, we know better. Starting with day one, your baby has a simple form of purposefulness.

CHAPTER 9

Parenting

Rules, Boundaries, Whining,
Demanding, Learning,
Social Behavior, and Punishing

The older your baby gets, the more the "self" emerges. You increasingly see your baby's personality come to light, which fills you with happiness. However, there are times when your child's interests are not the same as yours. Your child will test your limits, and it's up to you to set boundaries and teach your child rules, not to make life difficult for your child but because children need rules when growing up. By providing sensible rules, you're making sure that your child has a good start at the daycare center, in school, and later in life.

At what age do you have to set boundaries?

Once your baby has completed the leap of "principles" (64 weeks after the calculated due date or almost 15 months), you can and must teach your child rules. "Must" isn't a pretty word; however, it's appropriate. Children need to learn rules in order to be able to lead pleasant lives in society. In fact, children want to learn rules even though it doesn't seem like it with all the whining.

Can a baby under the age of 15 months learn rules?

Until the leap of "principles" has been accomplished, you can lead by example and correct your baby the moment they do something "wrong." You can, for example, say plainly, "No, don't do that!" when your baby pulls on you or when you take something away that your baby is not allowed to have. That way, you correct your little one in the course of the game they're playing. Be sure to enforce the rules immediately. Once the leap of "principles" is complete, children suddenly understand that they can get their way by acting very sweetly, by helping you, or, to the contrary, by whining. At this age, children already understand that certain behaviors can help them get what they want. That's when the time has come to lay down clear rules.

How can I keep my child from whining?

Every child whines, and it's simply part of life. One child may whine more than another. A vivacious child expresses their will more than a quiet child. However, disposition is not the only factor in determining whether your child will act like a little troublemaker every now and then. Your role is very important, too. If you don't take consistent action, your child will, no doubt, take advantage of it. When you don't take consistent action in setting rules it means that you forbid something sometimes but allow it at other times. It won't take your child long at all to figure out when something can be achieved with whining because you're emitting signals. By being consistent, you don't prevent your child's whining, but you're ensuring you reduce the frequency and length of the whining.

Sometimes the whining just doesn't stop. What do I do then?

At a first glance, enforcing the rules on a consistent basis seems easy. After all, adults know what's allowed and what isn't, and you would think it could be made clear to children, too. This is as far as theory goes. In reality, it's easy to be tempted to give in to a child's whining because other people are bothered by it, because you're in a hurry, or because you can't stand listening to it any longer. However, it is recommended to stay consistent, especially in these situations. If you give in just once, your child will remember and take advantage of you next time.

If all children whine anyway, what good does it do to enforce rules consistently?

Your child is at an age now where they are developing an increasingly stronger will. After the leap of "systems" (around the age of 17 months), they will experience that they are their own person with opinions and their own rights. That's a good development because children increasingly develop a sense of "self" that fits into society. Every human being is a social creature who wants to belong to a group and be respected by that group. A "sweet" child is more easily accepted than a "naughty" child, just to name two extremes. It's your job to raise your child to get along well with others; your child needs to be able to adapt within a group and know what's allowed and what isn't. Whining is normal and is part of your child's development, but don't let this be an excuse to refrain from taking action in the hope that it will pass on its own.

Is it possible to raise my child so they don't whine as they get older?

Your child will whine less if you only ask them to do what they're fully capable of doing from day one. That way, you subconsciously teach your child that you are expecting something from them. With every leap, your baby acquires a new perceptive ability, enabling your little one to do and understand something new.

This is your child's highest level of understanding at the moment. Once the leap has been accomplished, you may ask your child to use the enhanced perceptive ability. If you expect more from your child than the ability allows, your child will become frustrated and the task won't become easier. It will be quite the opposite; your child will whine more often and for longer.

How does my child always know exactly when whining works?

During the past months, you and your baby have become closer and closer. Once your child has reached the age between one to two years, your little one knows you inside and out. Your child knows exactly what you like, what's funny to you, and what you're sensitive to. Children at that age use this knowledge ruthlessly, no matter how pleasant-natured they are. A little one senses the exact moment you're tempted to give in. You must become aware of these moments. Think of the situations when you give in to your child's whining. Is it at the supermarket because you're embarrassed? Or is it when your child acts very sweetly and showers you with kisses? Or is it when you're busy cooking, your other children are making trouble, and the dog is looking at you with begging eyes? Once you're aware of when and why you break down, the danger of being caught off guard decreases, and you'll be able to react in time. For instance, you shouldn't allow your child to have their way while strangers are present because you're embarrassed of your child's behavior. You should react to your child's behavior instead of worrying about what the stranger thinks.

Should a babysitter enforce the same rules the parents set?

Being consistent is very important when it comes to parenting. Your 15-month-old child doesn't quite understand yet that Dad allows something that Mom doesn't allow. The message you're giving your child is that rules only apply in certain situations, so they will test to see if they can get away with it. This is too difficult for your child; you're asking too much of your little one. That's why it's best for you and your partner to agree to the rules and consistently enforce them. The same applies for the babysitter. Everyone in charge of raising your child has to be on the same page. This is the only way to be consistent.

When am I allowed to be more flexible with the rules?

Exceptions confirm the rule. However, exceptions also create confusion for your child. A child doesn't understand such subtleties of consistency until they're over two years old. At this time, you can explain that sometimes you make an exception to a rule, for example, allowing your child to have a snack at a party or to stay up longer on the weekends. Always clearly explain to your child that it's an exception. Tell your little one that something is allowed this once, and also explain why you're making an exception. Observe the way your child handles it. Does your child understand it's an exception, or does your little one start whining at you to gain more exceptions? Adjust the frequency you give exceptions based on your child's reactions.

What is the long-term effect of consistently enforcing the rules?

Teaching 15-month-old children the rules regarding what's appropriate and what isn't is one of the best premises to raise children who know and observe social values and standards. Children raised in this way will be self-confident when starting school and will fit in easily. The parents don't have to worry when their child goes to a friend's house to play because they know their child will behave. In short, the parents will be proud of their child. Children between the age of one and two years who haven't been taught rules whine more often and for longer periods of time than those that have been taught. It gets even worse at the age of four years and older. You can read many stories about aggressive children who throw tantrums, break things, and hurt others intentionally. These are the consequences when you don't take parenting seriously. And it's certainly not what parents wish for.

Is it okay to punish a baby?

Babies have no way of knowing that they are doing something "wrong." All you can say is "No, that hurts" or something along these lines and use facial expressions and reactions to make your displeasure clear. If your baby does the same thing again ten minutes later, repeat what you said earlier and show the same reaction. Babies don't understand what they're being punished for, and punishing babies would be inappropriate for that reason alone.

Starting from the age of 15 months, it's a different story. Children now understand that there are rules, and that they have to take responsibility for the consequences of testing the rules. Testing the rules by defying them multiple times is perfectly normal at this age. It is how children learn rules. If you'd like to "punish" your child because your little one is testing a rule, by no means should it be done in form of yelling, hitting, or by using any other form of physical or verbal force. By doing so, you only show your own weakness. However, you certainly may discipline your child at this age by showing your feelings and letting your little one feel that you don't accept the behavior. For instance, if your child takes a candleholder from the table, tell your child this is not allowed. If your child reaches for the candleholder again, then pick up your child and put them somewhere else in the room. Always tell your child at eyelevel why something is not allowed. Look at your child and try to distract your child afterwards with a different, "desirable" action.

How do I make it clear to a child that something is not allowed?

Words alone aren't enough, unfortunately, but neither are actions. You can tell your child a hundred times that climbing this or that is not allowed, but if you do so while laughing and with a friendly face while you stay seated on the couch, your protests won't make a big impression on your child, who will just carry on. Use verbal and nonverbal communication to make rules clear, including words, posture, and actions. It's about your facial expression and posture signaling in addition to verbally telling your child. Laugh when you're happy, and make an angry face when you're

irritated. This all sounds quite self-explanatory, but many people aren't aware of their expressions when they are talking. It's very important that your face and posture clearly show your current feeling, especially with a child. A little exaggeration doesn't hurt, either. Sometimes parents have to do a little bit of acting. Besides posture and facial expression, you also have to consider the level you're standing or sitting on. If you want your message to really get across, you need to look straight at your child. Get on the same eyelevel, and look them in the eye. That way, you drive the point home.

Sometimes, I have to laugh out loud when my child does something naughty. Is this wrong?

Fortunately, our children's behavior often makes us laugh, for example, when children try to do something secretly but it's completely obvious. Let's be honest; sometimes naughty behavior can be very amusing. Even whining may be downright funny. However, if you laugh, your child will interpret it to mean they are doing the right thing. Laughing means praising, so try to not laugh, no matter how difficult it may be. Also, ask your older children not to laugh when your baby misbehaves. Since it's even harder for children to suppress their laughter, tell them that it may be best for them to go to another room for a little while.

Can toddlers be aggressive?

Yes, toddlers can be aggressive. It's not unusual. Actually, almost all children at the age of one to two years show aggressive behavior. Of course, you have to understand the term "aggressive behavior" in the broadest sense. Generally, you'll notice children suddenly showing aggressive behavior more frequently after the leap of "principles" (around the age of 15 months). Examples of aggressive behavior might include a child biting something very hard, hitting something, or intentionally knocking something down and looking at you as if wanting to test you. That's exactly what your child is doing, they are not trying to make your life difficult, but after this leap they are experimenting with social behavior. Your child tries to judge whether their behavior is right or wrong by looking at your reaction. Your child is getting to know life, and you're there to teach your little one about life and the rules that come with it.

Do parents have any influence on aggressive behavior?

Every child experiments with aggression. Ninety percent of all 17-month-old children show occasional aggressive behavior. Most often, experimenting with aggression has topped out by the time children turn two, and it continues to decrease from that point on. Once your child starts elementary school, this phase is over or is at least, under normal circumstances it is. Although a certain degree of aggression is normal, it's never acceptable. Make this clear to your child, and always lead by example. If you yell and scream when arguing with your partner, you can't expect your child to solve conflicts any other way. When your child is angry, they will scream, too, and maybe even scream louder than you do. If you slam doors when you're angry, your child will probably throw things when they are angry. You're your child's role model, and you subconsciously teach your child how to act through your behavior. A child that grows up in a family where aggression is part of everyday life will continue this behavior when most other children don't show aggression anymore.

My child never whines when wanting something but is extremely sweet instead. How am I supposed to say "no?"

Some children find out early on that it's easier to catch flies with honey than with vinegar. They choose a different strategy other than whining to get their way. They look at you sweetly with big eyes, help you, and cuddle you; they play the sweet child. However, this behavior has the same purpose as whining. Both are methods for children to get their own way. The only difference is that whining is more annoying. Teach your child that some things are not allowed, no matter how nice they act. Rules are rules.

The Wonder Weeks Series

**The Wonder Weeks is a #1 worldwide bestseller
and a multi-award winning book!**

Over
2 million
copies
sold!

✓ Gives insight in baby's 10 major mental
developmental leaps

✓ Explains the fussy phases every child
experiences

✓ Shows when new skills can appear

✓ Gives parents tools to help their
baby through the fussy phases

✓ Offers parents support

➕ **GROUNDBREAKING** New research on sleep and leaps

My Wonder Weeks Diary

This luxury diary is your
ultimate keepsake. It is
based on a unique method
that enables you to track
the things that really matter.
A real must have!

The Best. Diary. Ever.